GOD
CREATED
NO BABY
SINNER(S)
FROM
ADAM

METUSELA ALBERT

To order additional copies of this book, contact:
Xlibris
844-714-8691
www.Xlibris.com
Orders@Xlibris.com

ISBN: Softcover   978-1-6641-7539-6
        EBook   978-1-6641-7538-9

Print information available on the last page

Rev. date: 05/28/2021

Contents

INTRODUCTION

Believe it or not? Most Protestant Churches and Mainline Denominations of the 21st century believed and preached that "Babies are Born sinners due to Adam's sin in us by inheritance."

That is a Satanic doctrine that excuses and immortalizes sin in the churches. Unfortunately, the Pastors and Church leaders will talk of overcoming sin by the blood of JESUS, but on the other hand, they promoted sin in the Churches in a very subtle (*sneaky, deceptive, and twisted*) way. Because you did not know it, hence I urge you to keep reading until the end. By the time you finished reading this book, you will not believe again in that Satanic doctrine.

HOW DID THEY EXCUSE AND IMMORALIZE SIN?

When they advocated that "Babies are born sinners due to Adam's sin in us by inheritance," they are indirectly teaching that it was GOD who created all human beings as adulterers, prostitutes, murderers, child molesters, rapists, robbers, drug addicts, drug cartels, idol worshippers, in their mother's womb at conception time.

In fact, they are putting the blame on God for creating them that way without their choice. They speak of the language – "We are what we are," "We are sinners because we are born sinners." They are taking no responsibility for their bad choices in transgressing God's law (Ten Commandments).

They also blamed their sin on Adam and said, "We are what we are from birth till death." Wow! That is a Satanic theology that permeated the so called - Christian Churches in the name of JESUS. The name of JESUS is taken in vain in this kind of theology.

They are also advocating that the reason we committed sin and are still committing sin is due to Adam's sin that we inherited without a choice. This kind of ideology justifies and excuses sin from the time a baby is conceived to the end of one's life. Thus, sin is immortalized in every baby that is born to this earth till the last baby before JESUS comes the second time to take the saints to heaven. In reality, this is a Satanic doctrine. And we as genuine professed Christians with a sound mind should confront, rebuke, and condemn such evil doctrines that make our loving Creator as the one who Created us as sinners from conception time till death. Spare not the rod.

ILLUSTRATION

Imagine, let's say someone goes to the shopping mall with a machine gun (M-15) and in less than 2 minutes, he kills 50 innocent people. Then later he goes to Court and tells the JUDGE, "I was born a killer (a murderer) due to Adam's sin in me." . . .

Surely, no sound minded Jury and Judge would acquit that stupid murderer to go free. If the killer goes free, based on that reason given, I can guarantee you that the public and the Media would become outraged and go after that stupid JUDGE. Common sense tells us that the JUDGE is stupid and is Satanic. A grade 10 student knows that the reason given by the murderer is hilarious and demonic.

But for those professed Christians who believed that evil theology that says, "We are born sinners due to Adam's sin in us by inheritance," they should uphold that JUDGE'S decision as a good verdict. They should not get angry with the murderer's reason and the JUDGE'S decision to acquit the killer.

Dear honest reader of this book, since you know that the JUDGE mentioned above in the illustration is wrong, then why are you believing in that false doctrine in your Church? Why are you believing in your Pastor who teaches that "babies are born sinners due to Adam's sin in us by inheritance"? . . .

Actually, those who believed that we are born sinners due to Adam's sin in us by inheritance, born killers, born prostitutes, born robbers, etc., should not be upset with the decision of the JUDGE.

AGAIN, I URGE YOU TO COME AND LET US REASON TOGETHER AND STOP THIS EVIL DOCTRINE FROM SPREADING IN YOUR CHURCH FROM TODAY.

IF you agreed that the JUDGE is 100% wrong by letting that killer go free, then WHY continue to believe in the false doctrine called – "Babies Are Born Sinners due to Adam's sin in us by inheritance," "Sin is by nature," "Sin is a state," "Sin is a condition," "Sin is what we are," "Sin is due to Adam's sin," "We inherited Adam's sin," etc.? Why? Why? Why?

Think folks. Think! Think! Think!

I believe that murderer SHOULD be convicted of an intentional criminal act, and SHOULD be jailed for life.

IF a silly illogical JURY of 9 people and the JUDGE allow that killer go free (not guilty), then expect more people to be killed. And expect the same reason from the same killer OR killer(s) in the next court hearing.

Expect banks, stores, and gas stations to be robbed because the robber will say, "I was born a robber due to Adam's sin in me."

Expect more girls to be raped because the rapist will say, "I was born a rapist due to Adam's sin in me."

This illustration is intended to draw your attention to re-look again into the false doctrine called – "We are born sinners due to Adam's sin in us by inheritance."

IF your mind is not aroused to see the *evilness* of that doctrine, then something is wrong somewhere, which is a sign that the Holy Spirit has departed and you are believing a Big lie without knowing it. Therefore, God will give you a delusion to believe a lie because you did not love the truth – (2 Thessalonians 2:9-11)

HERE'S THE THING. What is the teaching of your Church? . . . Is your Church teaching that false evil doctrine that makes God as the Creator of baby sinners? . . . It is time to challenge the false teachings of your Church without fear. It is time to leave the Church and go forward because you are not saved by the church. Remember, your denomination is <u>not</u> the Savior. Don't buy the lies of the Church anymore. Stop the spreading of that BIG LIE which is a PANDEMIC in the Churches.

....

THE BABYLONIAN CONFUSION IN THE MAINLINE DENOMINATIONS.

Most mainline denominations that existed today believed in the false and evil doctrine called "Babies are born sinners due to Adam's sin in us by inheritance."

Most Pastors of those churches believed it also because their Church teaches it. They have to keep their pay check coming from the Church. And some are ignorant to read the Scriptures in the context and reason logically to make sense of what they believed.

HOW DID THEY COME UP WITH THAT BELIEF?

1. First, they believed that after Adam and Eve sinned, their *"sinless nature"* became *"fallen sinful nature."*

2. They believed that *the fallen sinful nature* in itself is <u>equal</u> to sin.

3. Therefore, they believed that since we are all born with *the fallen sinful nature*, that makes us natural sinners at birth (conception time) due to Adam's sin in us.

4. That is how the belief about "Babies are born sinners due to Adam's sin" came about.

5. And now they have more false doctrines that existed from that one false doctrine.

6. For example, they teach the following false doctrines.

    (a) Sin is by the fallen sinful nature.

    (b) Sin is by birth.

    (c) All you have to do to be a sinner, is to be born.

    (d) Sin is inherited from Adam.

    (e) Sin is without your choice.

    (f) Sin is not by the transgression of the law, but by nature.

    (g) It is your fallen sinful nature that causes you to transgress the law.

    (h) Sin is a condition.

    (i) Sin is a state.

(j) Sin is universal (Universal Sinfulness) – (Everyone is a sinner because of Adam's sin in them).

(k) We will continue sinning till death since we have the fallen sinful nature from birth till death.

(l) Jesus could not have been born with the fallen sinful nature from virgin Mary because he would have become a natural sinner by nature.

(m) God's law cannot be kept by born again Christians because we are sinners by nature from conception time till death.

(n) Universal Salvation – Salvation is unconditional because JESUS died and saved you already at Calvary without your choice.

(o) All past, present, and future sins were forgiven at Calvary (31 A.D.).

(p) Sins before you committed were all forgiven at Calvary without your confession and repentance.

(q) The reason we obey God and keep his commandments is because we have already been forgiven and saved at Calvary.

(r) The reason we keep the Sabbath commandment is because we have been forgiven and saved at Calvary.

(s) The unrepentant Pharisees who killed JESUS at Calvary were forgiven unconditionally when JESUS died at 3 pm that Friday afternoon.

NOTE: ALL OF THE ABOVE FALSE DOCTRINES CAME OUT OF ONE DOCTRINE CALLED – THE FALLEN SINFUL NATURE IS SIN.

In this book, I will try and prove that the fallen sinful nature in itself is NOT equal to sin. Once you understood clearly that the fallen sinful nature is not equal to sin, then all those 12 other doctrines listed above from (a) – (s) are all wrong and should be condemned because they are ANTI-CHRIST teachings to make God as the Creator of Baby sinners from Adam.

Did you notice it? One error will always lead to another error and then many more errors to follow. One false doctrine expands to other false doctrines. The root evil doctrine is called – "The fallen sinful nature is sin in itself." This is the evil doctrine that expanded to the rest of those false doctrines listed above.

If you have been believing that "Babies Are Born Sinners due to Adam's sin in us by inheritance," I hope I have provoked your mind further to think because you have been brainwashed for so long. Your mind needs to be detoxed to get the toxic doctrines out in order for you to come to your senses. I once believed in those evil doctrines for many years, BUT not anymore.

Thank you for having an open mind to read this book. God bless.

CHAPTER 1

THE BIBLICAL DEFINITION OF SIN.

Scripture: 1 John 3:4 – (KJV)

[4] Whosoever committeth sin transgresseth also the law: <u>for sin is the transgression of the law.</u>

....

1 John 3:8 – (KJV)

[8] <u>He that committeth sin is of the devil;</u> for the devil sinneth from the beginning. For this purpose the Son of God was manifested, that he might destroy the works of the devil.

....

Let's summarize the text (1 John 3:4) in different points so that the truth becomes more outstanding and let it expose the error(s).

1. Sin has to do with the transgression of God's law.

2. In other words, the law has to exist <u>before</u> sin can exist.

3. The one who transgresses the law is the sinner. You are not a sinner because you are born – (1 John 3:4).

4. The law is good, holy, and righteous. There is nothing wrong or bad with the law – (Romans 7:12)

5. Sin has to be committed by a person to transgress the law. Therefore, sin is <u>a choice</u> by the transgressor.

6. Therefore, Sin is <u>not inheritable</u> from another person.

7. Without the transgression of the law, there is no sin – (Romans 4:15).

8. The sinner is <u>responsible</u> for the sin he or she committed.

9. Sin has to be committed by an individual person. Therefore, sin is <u>not universal</u> by one person.

10. Therefore, one person's transgression of God's law cannot make everyone a sinner without their choices.

11. Sin is not inheritable from Adam.

12. Sin is not transferable from Adam to his children.

13. If the definition of sin is not by the transgression of God's law, then sin can no longer become sin.

14. He or she that committeth sin is of the devil. This means, you cannot be a sinner by Adam's sin. Thus, you are not of the devil by Adam's sin. Adam's sin cannot make you become responsible for his sin.

15. Adam's sin cannot condemn you to die *the eternal death* (second death) without your choice.

16. Remember - You are not a sinner, a prostitute, an adulterer, a murderer, and idol worshipper, because of Adam's sin.

17. You must take responsibility for your choice to commit sin by transgressing God's law.

18. You must genuinely confess and repent of your sins committed by your own choice, then God will forgive you – (1 John 1:9; Proverbs 28:13; 2 Peter 3:9).

19. You cannot confess and repent for Adam's sins nor for the sins of another person – (Ezekiel 18:20).

NOTE: IF your Church is teaching "Babies Are Born Sinners due to Adam's sin in us by inheritance" AND "Sin is by nature," then you must do the right thing by rejecting your Church and turn away from that false teaching. Apparently, your church has become Satanic in teaching such false teachings which are ANTI-CHRIST. It is a Babylonian doctrine that confuses people in the Church. It immortalizes sin in the Church. It reveals the corruptness of the church.

Think! Think! Think!

///

THE BIBLICAL DEFINITION OF SIN

- **1 John 3:4** – Whosoever committeth sin transgresseth also the law; <u>for sin is the transgression of the law</u>.
  - ....
    - **Romans 4:15**
- ¹⁵ Because the law worketh wrath: for where no law is, <u>there is no transgression.</u>

Any definition of sin that contradicts the above is an attack on God's law to either abolish all Ten Commandments or part of the Ten. It is an attempt to excuse sin and immortalize sin in a subtle and deceptive way by Satan and his agents.

Prepared by: Metusela F. Albert

NOTE: REMEMBER, GOD'S LAW EXISTED IN HEAVEN BEFORE SIN CAN EXIST.

NO ONE CAN COMMIT SIN (TRANSGRESS THE LAW), IF THERE IS NO LAW THAT EXISTS TO TRANSGRESS – (Romans 4:15).

Please read this carefully and take time to understand it in the context of the law.

THE TRUE DEFINITION OF SIN

- 1 John 3:4 -9 - King James Version
- ⁴ <u>Whosoever committeth sin transgresseth also the law: for sin is the transgression of the law.</u>
- ⁶ <u>Whosoever abideth in him sinneth not</u>: whosoever sinneth hath not seen him, neither known him.
- ⁸ <u>He that committeth sin is of the devil</u>; for the devil sinneth from the beginning. For this purpose the Son of God was manifested, that he might destroy the works of the devil.
- ⁹ <u>Whosoever is born of God doth not commit sin</u>; for his seed remaineth in him: and he cannot sin, because he is born of God.
- ....
- Romans 4:15 - King James Version
- ¹⁵ Because the law worketh wrath: <u>for where no law is, there is no transgression.</u>

THE SATANIC ATTACK UPON JESUS AND HIS LAW.

- THE CORRECT DEFINITION OF SIN.

- 1 John 3:4 – King James Version
- Whosoever committeth sin transgresseth also the law: <u>for sin is the transgression of the law.</u>
- ....
- 1. Sin has to do with the breaking of God's Ten Commandments.
- 2. Sin is a choice by an individual.
- 3. Sin is <u>NOT</u> by another person.
- 4. Sin is <u>NOT</u> by birth.
- 5. Sin is <u>NOT</u> by nature.
- 6. Sin is <u>NOT</u> due to Adam's sin or Lucifer's sin.

- THE FALSE DEFINITION OF SIN

Sin is by the fallen sinful nature we inherited from Adam.

....

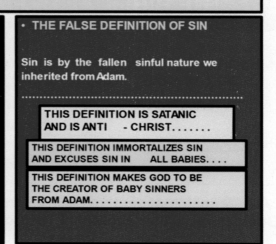

THIS DEFINITION IS SATANIC AND IS ANTI - CHRIST.......

THIS DEFINITION IMMORTALIZES SIN AND EXCUSES SIN IN ALL BABIES....

THIS DEFINITION MAKES GOD TO BE THE CREATOR OF BABY SINNERS FROM ADAM. ....

Prepared by: Metusela F. Albert

CHAPTER 2

THE ORIGIN OF SIN BY LUCIFER IN HEAVEN

Scripture:

Isaiah 14:12-14 – (KJV)

¹² How art thou fallen from heaven, O Lucifer, son of the morning! how art thou cut down to the ground, which didst weaken the nations!

¹³ For thou hast said in thine heart, I will ascend into heaven, I will exalt my throne above the stars of God: I will sit also upon the mount of the congregation, in the sides of the north:

¹⁴ I will ascend above the heights of the clouds; I will be like the most High.

Ezekiel 28:12-15 (KJV)

¹² Son of man, take up a lamentation upon the king of Tyrus, and say unto him, Thus saith the Lord God; Thou sealest up the sum, full of wisdom, and perfect in beauty.

¹³ Thou hast been in Eden the garden of God; every precious stone was thy covering, the sardius, topaz, and the diamond, the beryl, the onyx, and the jasper, the sapphire, the emerald, and the carbuncle, and gold: the workmanship of thy tabrets and of thy pipes was prepared in thee in the day that thou wast created.

¹⁴ Thou art the anointed cherub that covereth; and I have set thee so: thou wast upon the holy mountain of God; thou hast walked up and down in the midst of the stones of fire.

¹⁵ Thou wast perfect in thy ways from the day that thou wast created, till iniquity was found in thee.

EXPLANATION

Sin started in heaven by Lucifer. He wanted to be like God. Iniquity was found in his heart.

He transgressed the Ten Commandments in his heart / mind.

WHAT COMMANDMENT IN THE TEN COMMANDMENTS DID LUCIFER TRANSGRESS IN HEAVEN? . . .

He as a creature ought to worship God who created him. But when Lucifer wanted to be like God, he was coveting something that does not belong to him. Therefore, he transgressed commandment # 10 in the Ten Commandments.

He also transgressed commandment # 1 in the Ten Commandments which says, "Thou shalt have no other gods before me."

....

NOTE: Lucifer wanted to be like God. He did not want to be like the Son of God. This is an important point that needs understanding. There was no Son of God in heaven called JESUS at the time Lucifer and the angels sinned against God.

....

IF the Ten Commandments did not exist in heaven, then Lucifer could not have transgressed the law and become a sinner. Since the law existed in heaven, therefore, Lucifer's desire to be like God, revealed the sin (iniquity) in his heart.

Lucifer transgressed Commandment # 1 in the Ten Commandments. And one third of the angels in heaven followed him and rebelled against God. The angels also transgressed Commandment # 1.

Eventually, all of them were cast out of heaven to this empty planet earth of ours (Revelation 12:6-9) *before* God created our earth as in Genesis 1:1-31.

NOTE: Remember, Lucifer and 1/3 of the angels did not have a fallen sinful nature, yet they sinned against God in heaven. Thus, sin is the transgression of God's law. Sin is not by the fallen sinful nature.

I hope you who are reading this realize the greatness of this point that "sin is the transgression of God's law."

....

Remember, Lucifer and 1/3 of the angels did <u>not</u> have a fallen sinful nature, yet they sinned against God in heaven.

Therefore, sin is the transgression of God's law.

• Sin is <u>not</u> by the fallen sinful nature.

CHAPTER 3

THE ORIGIN OF SIN BY ADAM AND EVE ON EARTH.

Scripture:

Genesis 2:16-17 - KJV

[16] And <u>the Lord God</u> commanded the man, saying, Of every tree of the garden thou mayest freely eat:

[17] <u>But of the tree of the knowledge of good and evil, thou shalt not eat of it: for in the day that thou eatest thereof</u> thou shalt surely die.

....

EXPLANATION

When GOD created our planet earth, he made Adam and Eve on <u>the sixth day</u> of creation. Then GOD gave the warning to Adam and Eve in Genesis 2:16-17 before the seventh day (the Sabbath). At this time, the devil and his angels were already in our planet earth since the time they were cast out of heaven, but their presence in spirit form were not known to Adam and Eve.

Later, Lucifer tempted Eve at the Garden where the tree of the knowledge of good and evil. He spoke through the serpent as recorded in Genesis 3:1-4, and Eve did not know it was Lucifer, a fallen angel that spoke through the serpent. Eve believed it was the serpent that spoke to her. She was deceived. Adam believed his wife and ate the forbidden fruit since he saw that his wife after eating the fruit did not die as God said in Genesis 2:16-17. Eve and Adam lacked the faith in God's word and transgressed God's law.

IF Eve had believed what God said in Genesis 2:16-17, she would not have listened to the serpent nor eat of the forbidden fruit. She chose not to believe in God but in the serpent who spoke to her. Sad.

We do the same as what Eve did at times when we failed to trust in God in what he said and promised us in the Bible. We lack the faith and transgressed God's law. Many times, we find ourselves transgressing God's law because we lacked the faith to trust in what God had said in the written word in the Bible.

WHAT IS THE POINT?

Adam and Eve both ate the forbidden fruit – (Genesis 3:1-5). They transgressed God's law. At the time before Adam and Eve ate the forbidden fruit, they did not have a fallen sinful nature. Therefore, sin is the transgression of God's law – 1 John 3:4.

The fallen sinful nature is the _result_ of sin. This point must be understood well. You cannot define sin from the fallen sinful nature.

The biblical definition of sin is found in 1 John 3:4 – **"Sin is the transgression of the law."**

WHAT COMMANDMENT IN THE TEN COMMANDMENTS DID ADAM AND EVE TRANSGRESS?

Adam and Eve transgressed commandment # 1 which says, "Thou shalt have no other gods before me."

When Adam and Eve chose to believe the serpent's words and ate of the forbidden fruit, that revealed that they both have taken the serpent's words as more important to them as God's word, the Elohim (YAHWEH / JEHOVAH) who created them. Thus, they have another god.

They not only transgressed commandment # 1, but also transgressed commandment # 10 which says, "Thou shall not covet . . ."

Adam and Eve coveted the only one tree in the Garden that God commanded them not to eat. They had so many trees including the tree of life to eat, yet they ate the forbidden tree called the tree of the knowledge of good and evil.

LET'S REASON TOGETHER. SHALL WE?

Many people continue to believe in sin is by nature because they did not know that Adam and Eve transgressed the Ten Commandments. When you transgress one law, you then have transgressed all Ten. . . . (James 2:10). For example, when you abolished the seventh-day Sabbath Commandment, you then have abolished the law on adultery, kill, etc. It is that simple. You cannot tell us that the Sabbath commandment is only for the Jews, but the adultery commandment is for us. Adam and Eve were not Jews when the Sabbath commandment was given at creation week at the Garden of Eden – (Genesis 2:1-3).

Remember this – Sin cannot exist at all if the Ten Commandments did not exist. Sin is the transgression of God's law. It started in heaven by Lucifer and one third of the angels who transgressed commandment # 1 and commandment # 10. And repeated by Adam and Eve.

We are sinners because we have transgressed God's law. The fallen sinful nature does not make a person a natural sinner.

We are in need of a Savior (JESUS) to forgive our sins because we have transgressed His law.

We are not in need of a Savior (JESUS) because of our fallen sinful nature. Adam and Eve before they sinned (transgressed God's law) they did not need a Savior to forgive their sins. Only after they transgressed God's law that they needed a Savior. Thus, no baby is in need of a Savior to forgive his or her sins because the baby at conception time in the mother's womb has not transgressed God's law.

Folks, you know it yourself that the baby in the mother's womb did not know what is right from what is wrong. Did you not know that yet? Really? . . . Think! And stop fooling yourself as if you are that ignorant. This is not rocket science.

....

Remember, Adam and Eve sinned at the Garden of Eden. The y did <u>not</u> have a fallen sinful nature, yet they sinned against God on earth.

Therefore, <u>sin is the transgression of God's law</u> .

Sin is <u>not</u> by the fallen sinful nature.

CHAPTER 4

THE UNBIBLICAL DEFINITION OF SIN

When we know the truth, we will easily know the error. But if we don't know the truth, we will not know the error.

SO, WHAT IS THE TRUTH?

The true definition of sin is found in 1 John 3:4 – "Sin is the transgression of the law" There is only one law that we will all be judged by – (Ecclesiastes 12:13-14). It is the Ten Commandments. This law is not a Jewish law nor Moses' law.

THE UNBIBLICAL (FALSE) DEFINITION OF SIN IS:

1. The fallen sinful nature is sin.

2. Sin is by nature.

3. Sin is what we are.

4. Sin is by birth.

5. In order to be a sinner, all one has to do is to be born.

6. Sin is inherited.

7. Sin is without one's choice.

8. You are born a sinner due to Adam's sin in you.

9. Sin is a state.

10. Sin is a condition.

Those 10 expressions of sin listed above stemmed out of expression in # 1. The belief that the fallen sinful nature is sin in itself is the root cause of the other 9 expressions.

They are all evil expressions to justify and immortalize sin in all babies beginning from Adam and Eve's first child which is Cain to the last baby to be born before JESUS returns.

After Adam and Eve's fall into sin, we all inherited the fallen sinful nature. This a fact. However, the truth of the matter is – the fallen sinful nature is <u>not</u> sin.

CAUSE AND RESULT (EFFECT)

Sin is the transgression of God's law which is the <u>CAUSE</u>. But the fallen sinful nature is the RESULT; not the <u>cause</u>. This point has to be understood clearly from here.

IF this point is not understood, then you will end up believing that the fallen sinful nature is the <u>cause</u> for one to sin; and that would be like putting the CART in-front of the HORSE.

The Cart must always be <u>behind</u> the Horse.

....

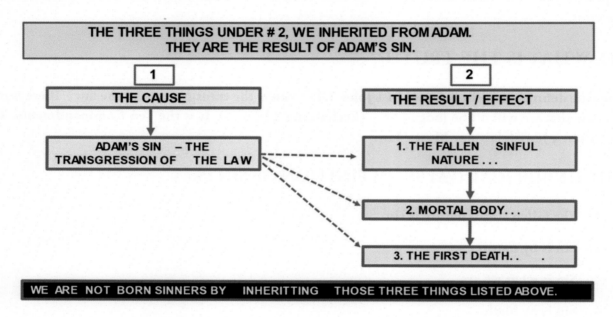

Prepared by: Metusela F. Albert

....

LET ME GIVE AN EXAMPLE <u>TO ILLUSTRATE</u> THE DIFFERENCE BETWEEN CAUSE AND RESULT (EFFECT) TO PROVOKE THINKING.

<u>Adultery is the sin</u> mentioned in the Ten Commandments (Exodus 20:14). This is commandment # 7.

<u>Adultery</u> is when a spouse has an affair with another person outside of the marriage. The result / effect which is the <u>consequences</u> of that bad decision made by whosoever, can bring about <u>divorce</u> to the couple.

Divorce is the <u>result (effect / consequences)</u>, <u>not</u> the sin. Divorce in <u>this context</u> is <u>not</u> the sin.

1. **It is <u>evil and Satanic</u> for the spouse who committed <u>adultery</u> by his or her own lust of the flesh to say, "I committed adultery because of Adam's sin in me."**

2. **It is <u>evil and Satanic</u> for the spouse who committed <u>adultery</u> by his or her own lust of the flesh to say, "I committed adultery because of my fallen sinful nature inherited from Adam."**

NOTE: When the reason for adultery is given as mentioned above, then adultery which is a sin becomes excusable. And sin becomes immortalized. Therefore, the sin of adultery is no more a sin. Then the law that defines sin is no longer in effect.

The bottom-line now is this. The Ten Commandments which is holy, just, and good - is abolished in a subtle way by that definition of sin which says, Sin is by the fallen sinful nature we inherited from Adam.

....

That is the UNBIBLICAL DEFINITION OF SIN which Satan instigated in the minds of the Pastors and mainline denominations to get rid of the true definition of sin written in 1 John 3:4 and Romans 4:15.

CAUSE AND EFFECT

- Adultery is the sin mentioned in Commandment # 7. When adultery takes place in a marriage situation, <u>divorce</u> is the result that follows .
- Divorce is the <u>result (effect / consequences)</u> , <u>not</u> the sin . Divorce in <u>this context</u> is <u>not</u> the sin.

1. It is <u>evil and Satanic</u> for the spouse who committed <u>adultery</u> by his or her own lust of the flesh to say, "I committed adultery because of Adam's sin in me."

1. It is <u>evil and Satanic</u> for the spouse who committed <u>adultery</u> by his or her own lust of the flesh to say, "I committed adultery because of my fallen sinful nature inherited from Adam ."

- NOTE: When the reason for adultery is given as mentioned above, then adultery which is a sin becomes excusable . And sin becomes immortalized. Therefore, the sin of adultery is no more a sin. Then the law that defines sin is no longer in effect.
- The bottom -line now is this . The Ten Commandments which is holy, just, and good - is abolished in a subtle way by that definition of sin which says, Sin is by the fallen sinful nature we inherited from Adam.

....

Dear husbands and wives, how would you feel or react to your spouse who returned home from work and told you that he or she had an affair with your sister or brother because he or she was born an adulterer due to Adam's sin.

Of course, you know it very well that God created no person an adulterer, a murderer, a robber, a sinner from Adam's sin.

God did **not** create your mother nor your wife an adulterer nor a prostitute nor a murderer. Think folks. . . . THINK! THINK! THINK!

We have been fooled for too long and it is time to turn away from such foolishness. We as Church Pastors have made the people to live in sin because of the Fundamental Beliefs of the Church.

THE IRONY BY THE PASTORS AND THE CHURCHES

While we as Pastors are calling upon the people to live holy and overcome sin by the blood of JESUS, yet at the same time we are telling them INDIRECTLY that we are born adulterers, prostitutes, fornicators, murderers, robbers, and we can commit unlimited adultery, sin, and yet still be saved by JESUS who loves us unconditionally.

What a contradiction! HOW long are we going to go on like this? This book is written for us to change our doctrines. We are to unite in the truth. We are not to unite in error.

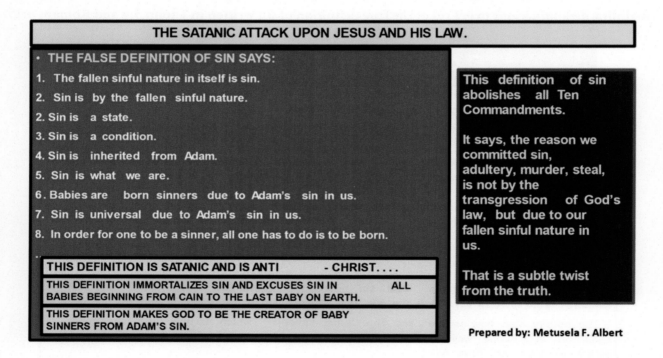

THE SATANIC ATTACK UPON JESUS AND HIS LAW.

- **THE FALSE DEFINITION OF SIN SAYS:**
1. The fallen sinful nature in itself is sin.
2. Sin is by the fallen sinful nature.
2. Sin is a state.
3. Sin is a condition.
4. Sin is inherited from Adam.
5. Sin is what we are.
6. Babies are born sinners due to Adam's sin in us.
7. Sin is universal due to Adam's sin in us.
8. In order for one to be a sinner, all one has to do is to be born.

THIS DEFINITION IS SATANIC AND IS ANTI   - CHRIST. . . .

THIS DEFINITION IMMORTALIZES SIN AND EXCUSES SIN IN   ALL
BABIES BEGINNING FROM CAIN TO THE LAST BABY ON EARTH.

THIS DEFINITION MAKES GOD TO BE THE CREATOR OF BABY
SINNERS FROM ADAM'S SIN.

This definition of sin abolishes all Ten Commandments.

It says, the reason we committed sin, adultery, murder, steal, is not by the transgression of God's law, but due to our fallen sinful nature in us.

That is a subtle twist from the truth.

Prepared by: Metusela F. Albert

CHAPTER 5

WE DID NOT INHERIT SIN FROM ADAM

SIN CANNOT BE INHERITED.

Scripture:

Ezekiel 18:20 – King James Version

²⁰ The <u>soul that sinneth</u>, <u>it shall die</u>. The son shall <u>not</u> bear the iniquity of the father, <u>neither shall the father bear the iniquity of the son</u>: the righteousness of the righteous shall be upon him, and the wickedness of the wicked shall be upon him.

According to the Scripture above, it says:

1. The <u>soul (person) that sins</u>, he or she shall die. (This death is <u>eternal death</u> which is the second death).

2. The <u>iniquity</u> (sin) of the father cannot be transferred to the son.

3. The <u>iniquity</u> (sin) of the son cannot be transferred to the father.

4. The <u>righteousness</u> of the father cannot be transferred to the son.

5. The <u>righteousness</u> of the son cannot be transferred to the father.

NOTE: The *death* mentioned in Ezekiel 18:20 is the *eternal death* which is the *second death*. This *death* is the wages of sin by the individual that is mentioned in Romans 6:23.

WHAT IS THE TRUTH ABOUT THE SIN BEARER?

All sins are *transferred* to JESUS alone who voluntarily became the Sin Bearer for Adam and Eve before Cain was born – (Genesis 3:15; John 1:29). Not one sin of Adam and Eve were transferred to

Cain and Abel nor to a baby. Not even one baby is born with Adam and Eve's sins. If this fact is not understood, then you are going to make GOD become the Creator of baby sinners from Adam's sin. Think folks!

NOTE: If the sins of Adam and Eve could be *transferred* to their children OR *inherited* by their children, then the death of JESUS at Calvary becomes null and void.

If Adam and Eve's sins were transferred *to Cain*, then Cain would have become the Sin Bearer for his parents.

If Adam and Eve's sins were transferred to *all babies*, then babies would have become Adam and Eve's Sin Bearer. And the gospel where JESUS alone is the Sin Bearer would have become null and void. Therefore, the death of JESUS at Calvary would mean nothing.

Dear folks, we must condemn the 11 false teachings listed below:

1. Babies are born sinners.

2. Sin is by nature.

3. Sin is by birth.

4. Sin is inherited from Adam.

5. Sin is without one's choice.

6. The moment the baby is conceived in the mother's womb, the baby is a natural sinner due to Adam's sin in us.

7. The fallen sinful nature is sin in itself.

8. In order for one to be a sinner, all one has to do is to be born.

9. Sin is what we are.

10. We are by what we are.

11. JESUS was not born with the fallen sinful nature like us because that would have made him a natural sinner in Mary's womb.

11 FALSE TEACHINGS ABOUT SIN

- These 11 false teachings listed below must be rejected and condemned :

1. Babies are born sinners.
2. Sin is by nature.
3. Sin is by birth.
4. Sin is inherited from Adam.
5. Sin is without one's choice.
6. The moment the baby is conceived in the mother's womb, the baby is a natural sinner due to Adam's sin in us.
7. The fallen sinful nature is sin in itself.
8. In order for one to be a sinner, all one has to do is to be born.
9. Sin is what we are.
10. We are by what we are.
11. JESUS was not born with the fallen sinful nature like us because that would have made him a natural sinner in Mary's womb.

PREPARED BY:Metusela F. Albert

THE SATANIC ATTACK UPON THE GOSPEL

- If Adam and Eve's sins were transferred to *all babies AND babies became sinners due to Adam and Eve's sins*, then babies would have become Adam and Eve's Sin Bearer. And the gospel where JESUS alone is the Sin Bearer for all mankind including Adam and Eve would have become null and void.

- Therefore, the death of JESUS at Calvary would mean nothing.

- Don't the Pastors, Churches, and Mainline Denominations of the 21st century (A.D.) realize how evil is their doctrine called "Babies Are Born Sinners due to Adam's sin " ?????? . . . .

Prepared by: Metusela F. Albert

JESUS WAS THE YAHWEH (JEHOVAH) WHO CREATED HEAVEN AND EARTH.

HE ALONE IS GOD.

HE CREATED NO BABY A NATURAL SINNER IN THE DEVIL'S IMAGE.

• **JESUS was the everlasting Father of the children of Israel in the OLD TESTAMENT who humbly incarnated into human flesh through Mary at Bethlehem and became the Son of God.**

• Isaiah 7:14;   9:6; 44:6, 24; 49:16; Matthew 1:21   -23; Luke 1:35.

CHAPTER 6

WE DID NOT INHERIT ETERNAL DEATH (THE SECOND DEATH).

SO, WHAT DID WE INHERIT FROM ADAM?

After Adam and Eve sinned, they lost immortality. Their immortality is conditional. As long as they obeyed God and not eat the forbidden fruit in the midst of the Garden (Genesis 2:16-17), hence, they would be allowed to continue to eat of the tree of life and live eternally. But if they sinned by eating the forbidden fruit, their nature would change from immortality to mortality, meaning – subject to death. This death is the first death because of the plan of Salvation that was made from eternity that YAHWEH himself would become the Sin Bearer and take the penalty of sin (wages of sin) in their place (substitute).

When they sinned, they were removed from the Garden of Eden, and an angel was stationed to guard *the tree of life* to avoid anyone eating it and become immortal sinners.

Unfortunately, professed Christians believed that Babies are born sinners from Adam. They did not realize that they have advocated a doctrine whereby sin is immortalized in a subtle way.

In fact, we did <u>not</u> inherit sin nor eternal death (second death) from Adam.

....

THESE ARE THE <u>THREE THINGS</u> WE INHERITED FROM ADAM.

1. The fallen sinful nature.

2. A mortal body.

3. The *first* death.

....

JESUS who became human flesh like us when he was born of Mary inherited those three things as well. He was <u>not</u> a sinner by the fallen sinful nature. That is the proof that no baby that is born with the fallen sinful nature is a natural sinner from Adam.

THREE THINGS WE DID <u>NOT</u> INHERIT FROM ADAM.

1. Sin

2. The <u>Second death</u> which is <u>eternal death</u>.

3. Immortality.

We did <u>not</u> inherit the sin of Adam because sin is by choice by an individual person. And we did <u>not</u> inherit the *second* death which is *eternal* death. And we also did <u>not</u> inherit immortality because God alone can change us from being mortal to immortality at his second coming. Immortality <u>cannot</u> be transferred from a person to another.

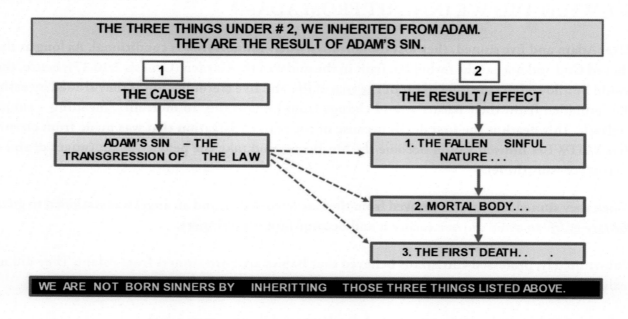

Prepared by: Metusela F. Albert

WE DID <u>NOT</u> INHERIT SIN FROM ADAM.

AND WE DID <u>NOT</u> INHERIT THE WAGES OF SIN WHICH IS ETERNAL DEATH (SECOND DEATH) FROM ADAM

CHAPTER 7

THE SIN BEARER FOR ADAM AND EVE.

The God who created Adam and Eve became the Sin Bearer for Adam and Eve immediately after they had sinned.

It is important that we read the Scriptures given below from Genesis 1:1 – 3:22 to learn of the God who created heaven and earth is not a Trinity God, but the Creator himself who voluntarily took the penalty of sin upon himself as the Sin Bearer.

The prophecy of YAHWEH himself to be born of a woman is alluded in Genesis 3:15. He will become the seed of the woman called Eve and later become a descendant of Abraham and King David through virgin Mary at Bethlehem.

....

Genesis 1:1 – In the beginning God created the heaven and the earth.

Genesis 1:26 - 27

26 And God said, Let us make man in our image, after our likeness: and let them have dominion over the fish of the sea, and over the fowl of the air, and over the cattle, and over all the earth, and over every creeping thing that creepeth upon the earth.

27 So God created man in his own image, in the image of God created he him; male and female created he them.

....

Genesis 2:7 -

7 And the LORD God formed man of the dust of the ground, and breathed into his nostrils the breath of life; and man became a living soul.

8 And the LORD God planted a garden eastward in Eden; and there he put the man whom he had formed.

....

Genesis 2:16-17

¹⁶ And <u>the LORD God</u> commanded the man, saying, Of every tree of the garden thou mayest freely eat:

¹⁷ But of <u>the tree of the knowledge of good and evil</u>, thou shalt not eat of it: for in the day that thou eatest thereof <u>thou shalt surely die.</u>

....

Genesis 3:9-11, 15, 22

⁹ And <u>the LORD God</u> called unto Adam, and said unto him, Where art thou?

¹⁰ And he said, I heard thy voice in the garden, and I was afraid, because I was naked; and I hid myself.

¹¹ And <u>he</u> said, Who told thee that thou wast naked? Hast thou eaten of the tree, whereof <u>I</u> commanded thee that thou shouldest not eat?

....

¹⁵ And <u>I</u> will put enmity between thee and <u>the woman</u>, and between thy seed and her seed; it shall bruise thy head, and thou shalt bruise his heel.

²² And <u>the LORD God said</u>, Behold, the man is become as one of <u>us</u>, <u>to know good and evil</u>: and now, lest he put forth his hand, and take also of the tree of life, and eat, and live for ever:

....

EXPLANATION

Yahweh (Elohim) who created Adam and Eve became the Sin Bearer immediately after their fall into sin. At this time after Adam and Eve's fall, Yahweh who is Jehovah did not have a Son called JESUS in heaven.

There is no such thing as God the Father had a Son in heaven called JESUS. In fact, JESUS was God the Father who created Adam and Eve and all things. He was not the Son of God then.

CATCH THIS POINT.

Yahweh himself became incarnated at Bethlehem through Mary and is called – JESUS, the Son of God – (Matthew 1:21-23; Luke 1:35).

Yahweh is Jesus. He was the Father of Adam and Eve and all who lived before the flood and after the flood in the Old Testament. And in the New Testament, he was still the father in heaven but incarnated into human flesh and dwelt on earth as if he was not an eternal God.

It was about 4,000 years after the fall of Adam and Eve that Yahweh (Jehovah) himself took human flesh through Mary at Bethlehem (04 B.C.) and died at Calvary (31 A.D.) at the age of 33 and a half years.

After Adam and Eve disobeyed God by eating the tree of the knowledge of good and evil, they immediately lost immortality. They became mortal beings, meaning, subject to death. This death is called the first death which is a sleep. They were allowed to live for a period of time then die. Adam lived 930 years, then died. That allowed Adam to live and able to see God's love in taking the eternal death in his place. That helped Adam to appreciate what God did by becoming the Sin Bearer for him, and he can confess and repent of his sins.

When JESUS took the penalty of sin which is eternal death from Adam, that did not mean Adam was forgiven immediately and given the gift of eternal life without having to condess his sins and repent. No! No! No! This must be understood well.

Genesis 3:15; John 1:29; 2 Corinthians 5:21.

CHAPTER 8

NO BABY WAS ADAM AND EVE'S SIN BEARER.

Scripture

Revelation 13:8 - King James Version

⁸ And all that dwell upon the earth shall worship him, whose names are not written in the book of life of the Lamb slain from the foundation of the world.

....

John 1:29 - King James Version

²⁹ The next day John seeth Jesus coming unto him, and saith, Behold the Lamb of God, which taketh away the sin of the world.

....

Ezekiel 18:20 (KJV)

²⁰ The soul that sinneth, it shall die. The son shall not bear the iniquity of the father, neither shall the father bear the iniquity of the son: the righteousness of the righteous shall be upon him, and the wickedness of the wicked shall be upon him.

....

After Adam and Eve sinned, it was JESUS who became their Sin Bearer. Their sins were transferred to JESUS alone. Of course, the innocent LAMB killed to atone for Adam and Eve's sins pointed to the incarnation of JESUS and his death at Calvary to pay for the whole world's penalty of sin including Adam and Eve.

....

- • **NO BABY WAS ADAM AND EVE'S SIN BEARER.**

- • **THEREFORE, NO SIN OF ADAM WAS TRANSFERRED TO A BABY.**

- • Scripture

- • Revelation 13:8   – (KJV)

- • [8] And all that dwell upon the earth shall worship him, whose names are not written in the book of life of the Lamb slain from the foundation of the world   .

- • ....

- • John 1:29   – (KJV)

- • [29] The next day John   seeth Jesus coming unto him, and saith,   Behold the Lamb of   God, which taketh away the sin of the world   .

- • ....

- • Ezekiel 18:20   - (KJV)

- • [20] The soul that   sinneth , it shall die. The son shall   not bear the iniquity of the father, neither   shall the father bear the iniquity of the son: the righteousness of the righteous shall be upon him, and the wickedness of the wicked shall be upon him.

- • ....

Read the previous Chapter (Chapter 7) and understand the truth that JESUS alone was the Sin Bearer for Adam and Eve before Cain, Abel, and Seth were born.

....

- • **IF THE SINS OF ADAM AND EVE WERE INHERITED BY ALL BABIES, THEN BABIES ARE NOW THE SIN BEARER FOR ADAM AND EVE.**

- • **WE NEED TO CONDEMN THIS TEACHING CALLED "SIN IS BY THE FALLEN SINFUL NATURE" AND "ALL BABIES ARE BORN SINNERS DUE TO ADAM'S SIN IN US BY INHERITANCE"**

BECAUSE IT HAS MADE THE ATONEMENT OF JESUS AT CALVARY NULL AND VOID.

CHAPTER 9

WE INHERITED THE FIRST DEATH FROM ADAM AND EVE.

THE DIFFERENCE BETWEEN THE FIRST AND THE SECOND DEATH.

The reality is, many Churches and Pastors still don't know the difference between the *first* and the *second* death. That is the reason they continued to believe that babies that died in an early stage of life is a natural sinner due to Adam's sin.

In fact, dying the first death is <u>not</u> the evidence that someone is a sinner. Whether you like it or not, we all inherited the *first death* without a choice. The first death is the evidence that Adam and Eve sinned, and that death is passed upon all of us to prove that death is the consequences of Adam and Eve's sin; not the wages of sin.

Eternal death (the second death) is the wages of sin – (Romans 6:23). When you commit sin *as an individual*, you will die the eternal death, if you chose <u>not</u> to believe in JESUS as your Sin Bearer and repent <u>not</u> – (1 John 1:9; Proverbs 28:13; 2 Peter 3:9).

NOTE: The *second* death comes at the end of the 1,000 years which is after the *second* resurrection. No one has died the second death yet because the return of JESUS, the first resurrection, the 1,000 years, and the second resurrection has not happened yet. These events must take place before the second death which is eternal death happens to the wicked.

Moses died the *first* death. He was resurrected and taken to heaven. He is now in heaven. Therefore, he will not die the second death. Moses was not a sinner because he died the first death. He became a sinner by choice when he transgressed God's law.

Enoch who lived before the flood was translated and taken alive to heaven. He is in heaven now. He was a sinner because he transgressed God's law. When he repented, God forgave his sins and translated him to immortality and took him to heaven. Therefore, he will not die the second death.

NOTE: JESUS is the only person that did not sin in his whole life, yet he had a fallen sinful nature. We all have sinned because we transgressed God's law. Babies that died early in life, they did not commit sin because they did not know right from wrong.

....

THERE ARE TWO RESURRECTIONS .

THE FIRST RESURRECTION IS FOR THE SAINTS, AND THE SECOND RESURRECTION IS FOR THE WICKED.

- **John 5:28 -29 (King James Version)**
- **28** Marvel not at this: for the hour is coming, in the which   **all that are in the graves shall hear his voice** ,
- **29** And **shall come forth** ; they that have done good, unto   **the resurrection of life** ; and they that have done evil, unto   the **resurrection of damnation** .

- THE FIRST RESURRECTION TAKES PLACE   AT THE SECOND COMING OF JESUS   BEFORE THE MILLENNIUM (1,000 YEARS).

- THE SECOND RESURRECTION TAKES PLACE AT   THE THIRD COMING OF JESUS   WITH THE NEW JERUSALEM CITY, AFTER THE MILLENNIUM (1,000 YERS).

- REVELATION 20:4-6; 21:1-7.

Prepared by: Metusela F. Albert

The Timeline Chart below shows that the Second Death will take place after the 1,000 years period which is marked by the Second Resurrection. . . . The Second Resurrection is the resurrection of the wicked.

In the first Resurrection, the saints are taken to heaven for a period of 1,000 years. They will live with God in heaven before returning with the New Jerusalem City at the 3RD coming of JESUS.

....

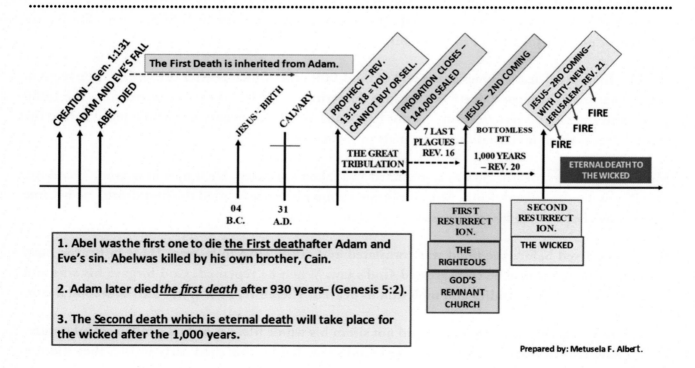

1. Abel was the first one to die the First death after Adam and Eve's sin. Abel was killed by his own brother, Cain.

2. Adam later died the first death after 930 years– (Genesis 5:2).

3. The Second death which is eternal death will take place for the wicked after the 1,000 years.

Prepared by: Metusela F. Albert.

THE 144,000 IN REVELATION 7:1-14 AND REVELATION 14:1-5.

The 144,000 sealed at the Close of Probation are <u>the righteous living</u> at the beginning of the Seven Last Plagues. They are the *righteous* that came out alive during the Great Tribulation period – (Revelation 7:1-3, 11-15).

During the time of the Seven Last Plagues, no one out of the <u>144,000</u> will experience the first death. The are not affected by the Seven Last Plagues.

Actually, the 144,000 is the <u>literal number of the righteous among those who are alive</u>. They are the ones to be <u>translated</u> like Enoch and be taken to heaven at the Second Coming of JESUS.

Those who are dead in Christ will be resurrected in <u>the first resurrection</u> - (1 Thessalonians 4:16-17). Abel who was killed by his brother Cain could be among this group, if he was not resurrected by JESUS when he resurrected others on that Sunday morning – (Matthew 27:51-54)

THE DIFFERENCE BETWEEN THE FIRST DEATH AND THE SECOND DEATH (ETERNAL DEATH).

- Again, <u>the timeline chart</u> below will show you clearly that God created no baby sinners from Adam. And the *first* death is <u>not</u> the evidence that a baby is born a sinner since *we all inherited the first death* from Adam. No one inherited *the second death* (eternal death) from Adam.
- The <u>second</u> death is a choice. And it is the wages (PENALTY) of sin for the individual person. You only become a sinner when you transgress God's law; <u>not</u> when you die the first death.

1. No person is a sinner by Adam's sin.
2. No person is a sinner by being born with the fallen sinful nature.
3. No person is a sinner by dying the first death during his or her lifetime.
4. No person inherited sin from Adam.
5. No person inherited <u>the second death</u> (eternal death) from Adam.
6. The <u>second death</u> is the wages (penalty) of sin by an individual who chooses to transgress God's law and repent not.
7. The <u>first death</u> is not the evidence that one is born a sinner.
8. We all inherited <u>the first death</u> from Adam, and the first death is only a temporary sleep; not the death of a sinner – (Romans 5:12).
9. When you transgress God's law, that is the time you become a sinner and in need of a Savior.
10. You are in need of a Savior / Sin Bearer when you transgress God's LAW – (1 John 3:4).

Author: Metusela F. Albert

CHAPTER 10

THE FIRST DEATH IS NOT THE EVIDENCE THAT ONE IS BORN A SINNER.

When a baby dies by abortion, or premature death, or during delivery time, or after being born, that does not prove that the baby is a sinner. No baby is a sinner by dying the first death.

No baby is a sinner by Adam's sin. The fallen sinful nature does not make a person a sinner.

Even adults who died by an accident or by sickness or by old age, that first death is not the evidence that one is born a sinner.

GOD who created us in his own image made no baby sinners from Adam's sin.

Again, the timeline chart below will show you clearly that God created no baby sinners from Adam. And the *first* death is not the evidence that a baby is born a sinner since *we all inherited the first death* from Adam. No one inherited the second death (eternal death) from Adam.

The *second* death is a choice. And it is the wages (PENALTY) of sin for the individual person. You only become a sinner when you transgress God's law; not when you die the first death.

1. No person is a sinner by Adam's sin.

2. No person is a sinner by being born with the fallen sinful nature.

3. No person is a sinner by dying the first death during his or her lifetime.

4. No person inherited sin from Adam.

5. No person inherited the second death (eternal death) from Adam.

6. The second death is the wages (penalty) of sin by an individual who chooses to transgress God's law and repent not.

7. The first death is not the evidence that one is born a sinner.

8. We all inherited <u>the first death</u> from Adam, and the first death is only a temporary sleep; not the death of a sinner – (Romans 5:12).

9. When you transgress God's law, that is the time you become a sinner and in need of a Savior.

10. You are in need of a Savior / Sin Bearer when you transgress God's LAW – (1 John 3:4).

....

WHAT IS THE DIFFERENCE BETWEEN THE DEATH OF A BABY AND THE DEATH OF ONE WHO KNEW RIGHT FROM WRONG?

Both died *the first death* only. This is a truth that many people and churches still don't know yet. That is the reason they still believe in Babies are born sinners.

The baby that died at an early age did not commit sin. But the person who passed the age of accountability who knew right from wrong in which God knows, he or she is a sinner sometime in his or her life.

Therefore, at the time of his or her death after the age of accountability, that person may be still an unrepentant sinner or a repentant sinner. God alone knows. An unrepentant sinner will not be saved. But a repentant sinner in the LORD will be forgiven and resurrected in *the first resurrection* to eternal life when JESUS returns the second time – (1 Thessalonians 4:16-17).

We who are alive know that we will die. And that death is called *the first death* which is a sleep.

THE SECOND DEATH WHICH IS ETERNAL DEATH WE DID NOT INHERIT FROM ADAM.

The *the unrepentant sinner* will die *the first death* as well as *the second* death which is also called <u>eternal death</u>. The second death *takes place after* the second resurrection. The *second death* is the death for the unrepentant sinners; those who rejected JESUS and his commandments.

Satan and his angels will be destroyed eternally by fire during this time after the second resurrection. (See the timeline Chart provided).

THIS CHART IS HELPFULF TO SEE THE FIRST AND SECOND RESURRECTIONS.

IT ALSO SHOWS <u>THE SECOND DEATH</u> WHICH COMES AFTER THE SECOND RESURRECTION.

....

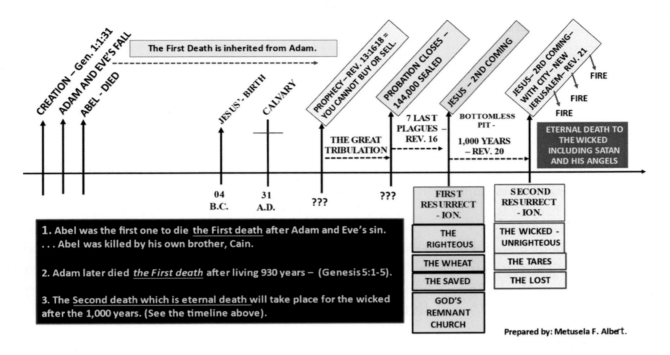

1. Abel was the first one to die <u>the First death</u> after Adam and Eve's sin. . . . Abel was killed by his own brother, Cain.

2. Adam later died <u>*the First death*</u> after living 930 years – (Genesis 5:1-5).

3. The <u>Second death which is eternal death</u> will take place for the wicked after the 1,000 years. (See the timeline above).

Prepared by: Metusela F. Albert.

....

The *<u>first death</u>* is the <u>result</u> of Adam and Eve's sin; not the result of your sin. Don't miss this important point.

....

THERE ARE TWO RESURRECTIONS .

THE FIRST RESURRECTION IS FOR THE SAINTS, AND THE SECOND RESURRECTION IS FOR THE WICKED.

- **John 5:28 -29 (King James Version)**
- 28 Marvel not at this: for the hour is coming, in the which <u>all that are in the graves shall hear his voice</u> ,
- 29 And <u>shall come forth</u> ; they that have done good, unto <u>the resurrection of life</u> ; and they that have done evil, unto <u>the resurrection of damnation</u> .

- THE FIRST RESURRECTION TAKES PLACE <u>AT THE SECOND COMING OF JESUS</u> <u>BEFORE</u> THE MILLENNIUM (1,000 YEARS).

- THE SECOND RESURRECTION TAKES PLACE AT <u>THE THIRD COMING OF JESUS</u> WITH THE NEW JERUSALEM CITY, AFTER THE MILLENNIUM (1,000 YERS).

- REVELATION 20:4-6; 21:1-7.

Prepared by: Metusela F. Albert

SINLESSNESS AND IMMORTALITY ARE NOT THE SAME THING.

Born again Christians can be holy and sinless, yet not immortal. For example, JESUS who was born with the fallen sinful nature from Mary, lived a life without sin. In human flesh through Mary, he was tempted in all points as we are, yet sinned not (Hebrews 4:15),

In humanity, JESUS was sinless, but he was not immortal. It was after his resurrection that his mortal body changed to immortality. He ascended to heaven with his immortal body that had the nail prints on his hands.

An immortal body means, a non-perishable body. Death cannot destroy that body that is immortal. In fact, the second death after the millennium (1,000 years) which is the wages of sin has no power over that immortal body. Those who are not changed to immortality like the twinkling of an eye at the second coming of JESUS will die the second death (the eternal death).

The wicked whom Jesus will resurrect at the second resurrection are not changed to immortality. They will die the second death. (See the Timeline Chart below}.

....

BORN AGAIN CHRISITANS

When you are born of God, you can be sinless (1 John 3:6-9), but not immortal yet until JESUS returns the second time to change you into immortality and take you to heaven –

(1 Thessalonians 4:16-17; 1 Corinthians 15:52-55).

//

PLEASE SEE THE TIMELINE CHART BELOW WHERE IT SHOWS THE FIRST RESURRECTION AND THE SECOND RESURRECTION WHICH ALSO SHOWS THE TIME OF ETERNAL DEATH WHICH IS THE SECOND DEATH.

ETERNAL DEATH WILL TAKE PLACE AFTER THE SECOND RESURRECTION. SATAN AND HIS WICKED ANGELS WILL BE DESTROYED AT THIS TIME AS PER GOD'S PLAN.

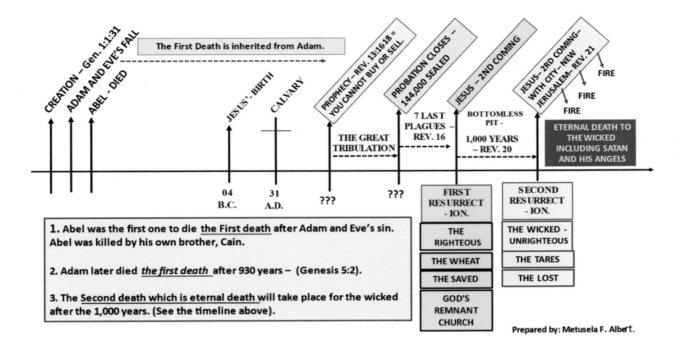

1. Abel was the first one to die the First death after Adam and Eve's sin. Abel was killed by his own brother, Cain.

2. Adam later died the first death after 930 years – (Genesis 5:2).

3. The Second death which is eternal death will take place for the wicked after the 1,000 years. (See the timeline above).

Prepared by: Metusela F. Albert.

THE TRUTH IS ALWAYS THE TRUTH, WHETHER YOU BELIEVED IT OR NOT.

The Timeline Chart above shows the overall plan of Salvation for mankind when God cast out from heaven the devil and his angels to our empty planet earth before he created our earth in Genesis 1:1-31. God who is omniscient (all knowing) had a foreknowledge that Adam and Eve whom he had not created yet, will fall into sin when tempted by the serpent at the Garden of Eden.

Therefore, God reserved the devil and his angels to be destroyed after the millennium (1,000 years). And the wicked descendants of Adam and Eve will also be destroyed at the same time. God's plan is far to greater than what we think. Try and look at the Chart above and recognize God's plan written in the Scriptures. Wow!

Fire from heaven will destroy them. It is not an eternal fire that keeps burning and burning for eternity. After being burned up, God will renew this earth and place the city called New Jerusalem on earth (Revelation 22). The saints will live on this earth and JESUS will be their God – (Revelation 21:6-7).

There will be no more sin, no more death, no more pain, no more suffering, no more crying, in the New earth. No more Pandemic.

Therefore, the first death is not the end of life. There is the assurance of eternal life in JESUS after the first death – (1 Thessalonians 4:16-17).

THE FIRST DEATH IS NOT THE EVIDENCE THAT A BABY IS BORN A SINNER.

GOD CREATED NO BABY SINNERS FROM ADAM

- PART 2

CHAPTER 11

YAHWEH (JESUS) WHO CREATED THE LIGHT LATER INCARNATED INTO HUMAN FLESH.

Why is this Chapter so important that we should understand our God who created the light?

Because the God who created the light created Adam and Eve and all mankind. And later he became human flesh by incarnation through Mary at Bethlehem and died at Calvary as our Sin Bearer. He took humanity with the fallen sinful nature like us, yet not a sinner by nature. That is the whole point to prove that babies are not sinners by the fallen sinful nature. We must be able to connect the dots of every Chapter designed in this Book to enlighten a world that is so full of darkness in regard to this subject of sin.

Yahweh (Jehovah) who created heaven and earth became the Messiah and is called JESUS of Nazareth. He humbly incarnated into human flesh like us with the fallen sinful nature through Mary at Bethlehem and became the Son of God in order to die at Calvary to pay for the penalty of sin, to give us an opportunity to have eternal life. What an amazing love.

//

NO BABY THAT IS BORN WITH THE FALLEN SINFUL NATURE IS A NATURAL SINNER BECAUSE JESUS HIMSELF WAS BORN WITH THE FALLEN SINFUL NATURE HE INHERITED THROUGH MARY AT BETHLEHEM, YET NOT A SINNER BY NATURE.

If you failed to understand this incarnation process that JESUS took to pay for the penalty of sin at Calvary, then your gospel about JESUS will become a distorted and corrupt gospel.

The God who created the light in Genesis 1:3 is the same God who spoke to prophet Isaiah and all the other prophet in the Old Testament.

Please read the information in the four Scriptures given below.

Isaiah 43:10
Isaiah 44:6, 24
Isaiah 49:16.

You cannot miss not to understand those Scriptures.

THE GOD WHO SPOKE TO PROPHET ISAIAH IS THE ONLY ONE GOD IN HEAVEN.   HE IS JESUS!

- Isaiah 43:10
- 10 Ye are my witnesses, saith the   LORD , and my servant whom I have chosen: that ye may know and believe me, and understand   that I am he: before me there was no God formed, neither shall there be after me.

  THE REDEEMER

- Isaiah 44:6
- 6 Thus saith   the LORD the King of Israel, and his redeemer   the LORD of hosts; I am the first, and I am the last; and   beside me there is no God   .

  THE CREATOR

- Isaiah 44:24
- 24 Thus saith the   LORD , thy redeemer   , and he that formed thee from the womb   , I am the LORD that maketh   all things; that stretcheth   forth the heavens   alone; that spreadeth   abroad the earth by   myself;

- Isaiah 49:16   **THE PROPHECY OF HIS DEATH AT CALVARY**
- 16 Behold, I have graven thee upon the palms of my hands   ; thy walls are continually before me.

DID YOU NOT KNOW YET?

- It was YAHWEH (JEHOVAH) who became human flesh at Bethlehem and is called – the Son of YAHWEH.

- It was NOT the Son of YAHWEH who became human flesh. . . .

- In fact, YAHWEH did not have a Son called JESUS in heaven. JESUS was YAHWEH before the incarnation through virgin Mary at Bethlehem.

A FUNADAMENTAL TRUTH

Our Creator did <u>not</u> create one baby in the image of the devil - a sinner, a murderer, a prostitute, an adulterer, an idol worshipper, a robber, a drug addict, a drunkard, a fornicator, etc.

Once you understood this fundamental truth well, you then will not believe again in the 11 false doctrines listed.

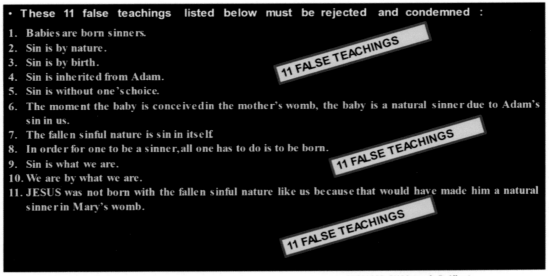

- These 11 false teachings listed below must be rejected and condemned :
1. Babies are born sinners.
2. Sin is by nature.
3. Sin is by birth.
4. Sin is inherited from Adam.
5. Sin is without one's choice.
6. The moment the baby is conceived in the mother's womb, the baby is a natural sinner due to Adam's sin in us.
7. The fallen sinful nature is sin in itself.
8. In order for one to be a sinner, all one has to do is to be born.
9. Sin is what we are.
10. We are by what we are.
11. JESUS was not born with the fallen sinful nature like us because that would have made him a natural sinner in Mary's womb.

11 FALSE TEACHINGS

11 FALSE TEACHINGS

11 FALSE TEACHINGS

PREPARED BY:Metusela F. Albert

CHAPTER 12

JESUS TOOK A MORTAL BODY LIKE US DURING HIS INCARNATION.

Scripture: Luke 23:44-56.

[44] **And it was about the sixth hour, and there was a darkness over all the earth until the ninth hour.**

[45] And the sun was darkened, and the veil of the temple was rent in the midst.

[46] And when Jesus had cried with a loud voice, he said, Father, into thy hands I commend my spirit: and having said thus, **he gave up the ghost.**

[47] Now when the centurion saw what was done, he glorified God, saying, Certainly this was a righteous man.

....

[50] And, behold, there was a man named Joseph, a counsellor; and he was a good man, and a just:

[51] (The same had not consented to the counsel and deed of them;) he was of Arimathaea, a city of the Jews: who also himself waited for the kingdom of God.

[52] **This man went unto Pilate, and begged the body of Jesus.**

[53] And he took it down, and wrapped it in linen, and laid it in a sepulchre that was hewn in stone, wherein never man before was laid.

[54] **And that day was the preparation, and the sabbath drew on.**

[55] **And the women also, which came with him from Galilee, followed after, and beheld the sepulchre, and how his body was laid.**

[56] **And they returned, and prepared spices and ointments; and rested the sabbath day according to the commandment.**

EXPLANATION

The Roman soldiers killed Jesus by crucifying him on a cross at Calvary on a Friday afternoon <u>before the weekly Sabbath day</u>.

If JESUS did not have a mortal body, then he could not have been tortured and killed by the Romans soldiers at Calvary. It is that simple.

//

- If JESUS did not have a mortal body like us, then he could not have been tortured and killed by the Roman soldiers at Calvary.

- This is   <u>another evidence</u>   that Babies are <u>not</u> born sinners because JESUS in his incarnation process took up a <u>mortal body</u> with <u>a fallen sinful nature through</u> Mary at Bethlehem, yet not a sinner by nature.

CHAPTER 13

JESUS TOOK THE FALLEN SINFUL NATURE OF ADAM THROUGH MARY.

Scripture:

Hebrews 2:14-17

[14] Forasmuch then as the children are partakers of flesh and blood, he also himself likewise took part of the same; that through death he might destroy him that had the power of death, that is, the devil;

[15] And deliver them who through fear of death were all their lifetime subject to bondage.

[16] **For verily he took not on him the nature of angels; but he took on him the seed of Abraham.**

[17] **Wherefore in all things it behoved him to be made like unto his brethren,** that he might be a merciful and faithful high priest in things pertaining to God, to make reconciliation for the sins of the people.

....

Hebrews 4:15

[15] **For we have not an high priest which cannot be touched with the feeling of our infirmities; but was in all points tempted like as we are, yet without sin.**

....

JESUS was tempted like as we are, yet did not sin.

JESUS was tempted in all things as we are because he took up a fallen sinful nature in his incarnation through Mary. But the fallen sinful nature did not make JESUS a sinner by birth.

JESUS, in humanity, would have become a sinner, if he had succumbed to temptations and transgressed the Ten Commandments.

He could not have been tempted as we are if he did not have a fallen sinful nature like as we are.

The fallen sinful nature does not make a person a natural sinner at conception time. If sin is by the fallen sinful nature, then JESUS who was born with the fallen sinful nature like us through virgin Mary would have become a sinner by birth.

THIS IS A FUNDAMENTAL TRUTH THAT NEEDS TO BE UNDESTOOD

Since JESUS was born with the fallen sinful nature, yet not a sinner by the fallen sinful nature, therefore, all babies that are born with the fallen sinful nature are not born sinners.

Again, no baby that is born with the fallen sinful nature is born a sinner since Jesus was born with the fallen sinful nature, yet not a sinner.

Sin is the transgression of God's law – 1 John 3:4. But the fallen sinful nature is the *result* of sin. The result is *not* the cause of sin.

....

COME AND LET'S REASON TOGETHER AND THINK LOGICALLY ON THIS ISSUE OF SIN AND THE FALLEN SINFUL NATURE.

Lucifer and one third of the angels in heaven sinned against God. They transgressed God's law in heaven and became sinners. They did **not** have a fallen sinful nature while in heaven, yet sinned. Therefore, sin is **not** by the fallen sinful nature. **Think! Think! Think!**

Again, Adam and Eve did **not** have a fallen sinful nature until after they disobeyed God and ate of the forbidden fruit. The fallen sinful nature is the **result** of their transgression of God's law. Therefore, sin is **not** by the fallen sinful nature. **Think! Think! Think!**

....

- If JESUS did not have a mortal body like us, then he could not have been tortured and killed by the Roman soldiers at Calvary.

- This is __another evidence__ that Babies are __not__ born sinners because JESUS in his incarnation process took up a mortal body with a fallen sinful nature through Mary at Bethlehem, yet not a sinner by nature.

- •

- NO BABY THAT IS BORN WITH THE FALLEN SINFUL NATURE IS A NATURAL SINNER BECAUSE JESUS HIMSELF WAS BORN WITH THE FALLEN SINFUL NATURE HE INHERITED THROUGH MARY AT BETHLEHEM, YET NOT A SINNER BY NATURE.

- If you failed to understand this incarnation process that JESUS took to pay for the penalty of sin at Calvary, then your gospel about JESUS will be a distorted gospel and will reveal the evil corruptness of your doctrine.

- Writte n by: Metusela F. Albert, Author of the Book, __God created No Baby Sinners from Adam__ .

CHAPTER 14

THE <u>TWO NATURES</u> OF JESUS (DIVINE AND HUMAN) WHILE IN HUMAN FLESH ON EARTH.

Many people who professed to believe in JESUS as the Messiah still do not understand the two natures Jesus had while in human flesh on earth for thirty-three and a half years.

EXPLANATION

In the Old Testament, JESUS was the Almighty God of Abraham who created heaven and earth. He was the Elohim (YAHWEH / JEHOVAH) who created light in Genesis 1:3. He created Adam and Eve on the sixth day. And he rested on the seventh day after making heaven and earth in six days. (Genesis 1:1-3, 26-27; 31; 2:1-3).

He was the Almighty God of Abraham who spoke to Moses at the burning bush. He was called I am that I am. (Exodus 3:13-14; John 8:56-58).

He was the God of prophet Isaiah called – The King of the Jews, the First and the Last, the Redeemer of Israel. (Isaiah 44:6, 44; 49:16).

Further reading - John 5:39, 46; Revelation 21:6-7.

....

When **YAHWEH** humbly took human flesh through Mary by incarnation, <u>he did not cease</u> from being God. In fact, he humbly became human flesh and took up the fallen sinful nature of man. He had the second nature which is humanity. Therefore, JESUS had the divine and the human nature in himself.

As a divine being, JESUS knew the end from the beginning. But as a human being like us, he did not know the future.

As a divine being, He was the God of Abraham. But as a human being like us, he was born of Mary and was tortured by the Romans at Calvary and died.

When JESUS died at Calvary, it was his **mortal human nature** that died; **not** his divine nature. For his divine nature is immortal and cannot die. God is eternal and has no beginning and no ending. He is the Alpha and Omega.

LET'S REPEAT THE POINT AGAIN FOR THE SAKE OF THOSE WHO FIND IT DIFFICULT TO UNDERSTAND THIS SUBJECT ABOUT JESUS CHRIST'S INCARNATION INTO HUMAN FLESH.

When in human flesh, YAHWEH was still God. He appeared to the Jews as a human being only since he veiled his divine nature. No mortal being can see JESUS in his divine nature and be alive.

Remember, the Jews saw JESUS as only human, and that is why they killed him became JESUS claimed to have power to forgive sins. The Pharisees said, God alone can forgive sin. Of course, only God can forgive sins. They did not realize that JESUS is God also. They claimed to understand the Scriptures, but in reality, they did not.

....

THE <u>TWO NATURES OF JESUS</u> WHILE IN HUMANITY ON EARTH.

Many people who professed to believe in JESUS as the Messiah still don't understand the INCARNATION step YAHWEH took to become human flesh through Mary at Bethlehem.

That is the reason they continue to believe in the Trinity doctrine called – three persons make up one God.

And that is why they continue to believe that JESUS was the Son of God the Father in heaven because they did not know that JESUS was God the Father in heaven at the time of creation.

....

Prior to JESUS CHRIST'S incarnation into human form through Mary at Bethlehem, He was ***the only self*-existent God** who lived in heaven from eternity. He alone created heaven and earth.

1.   THE PLAN OF SALVATION IMPLEMENETED BY THE CREATOR

After Adam and Eve's fall, the plan of salvation was implemented by JESUS who created heaven and earth – (Genesis 3:11-15). Now, He would have to be incarnated and be born through a virgin woman called Mary to be mankind's Sin Offering to pay the penalty of sin, <u>the second death</u> which is eternal death. About four thousand years after the fall of Adam and Eve, JESUS finally arrived at Bethlehem, as prophesied - (Genesis 3:15; Revelation 13:8; Isaiah 7:14; 9:6; Micah 5:2; Matthew 1:21-23).

2.   THE CREATOR WAS PROPHESIED TO BE THE MESSIAH, THE SON OF GOD IN HUMAN FLESH.

In eternity, God planned the creation of the world and the plan of salvation for mankind since he had foreknowledge of the angels' fall in heaven, and Adam and Eve's fall on earth. He alone did the creation of heaven and earth – The Creator of the heaven and the earth was **JEHOVAH (YAHWEH)** who later became human flesh through Mary at Bethlehem at 04 B.C., and is called *JESUS, the Son of God* – (Luke 1:35).

HE became the MESSIAH at His baptism (27 A.D.) when the Holy Spirit anointed him – (Matthew 3:16-17; Luke 3:22-24), and confirmed by the Father's voice from heaven. JESUS in spirit form was the Father who spoke from heaven and said, "This is my beloved Son in whom I am well pleased." JESUS was the God of Abraham in human flesh in Jordan river baptized by John. The Holy Spirit is the Spirit of God who came upon Jesus in human flesh.

3.   THE REASON THE CREATOR HAD TO BE INCARNATED

Since **JESUS** was the <u>**everlasting God**</u>, **the Creator** of heaven and earth, He cannot be born nor die. Therefore, He had to go through the *incarnation process* to allow Him to become human like us, to enable Him to die at Calvary as mankind's Sin Bearer.

When **JESUS** was born, He ***did not cease*** from being God. He ***did not cease*** from being JEHOVAH. He ***did not cease*** from being the God of Abraham, Isaac, and Jacob. He ***did not cease*** from being the <u>**"I AM THAT I AM"**</u> who spoke to Moses at the burning bush. He ***did not cease*** from being the God of the prophets in the Old Testament.

While in human flesh, **JESUS** *did* not cease to be God – (Exodus 3:13-14; John 8:58). He still has the divine power, the creative power; but He ***did not*** use it to overcome sin for His own benefit. He veiled his glory because no man can see him as God and still be alive. He appeared on earth as a servant in human flesh; not as an eternal God. He appeared on earth as a descendant of Abraham to prove that man can live a holy life by dependency upon God the Father's power.

He humbly took up ***the role of the Son of God*** in the New Testament – (Luke 1:35; John 5:39, 46). But in the Old Testament, He was called – **"Wonderful, Counselor, Mighty God, Everlasting Father, Prince of Peace, Immanuel"** – (Isaiah 9:6; 7:14). He was also called **the first and the last, the king of the Jews, the Redeemer, the Creator** – (Isaiah 44:6, 24; 48:12-13; 63:16).

He later took up the human form like us – (Hebrew 2:14-17; Philippians 2:5-8; Romans 8:3). He became **mortal** and had ***a fallen sinful nature***, similar to ours. He was tempted in all things like as we are, yet never sinned. He lived a life without sin to prove that sin cannot be excused – (Hebrews 4:15). He is our example – (2 Peter 2:21-23). He has the authority and power to forgive sins because He did not cease from being God. He forgave the sins of the paralytic, and the Pharisees who were present in the house called Him a Blasphemer – (Mark 2:1-10). The Pharisees said in their minds, "God alone can forgive sins." Those Pharisees ***did not*** realize that JESUS was the God who delivered their forefathers from slavery in Egypt (Exodus 20:1-3).

4. HE MYSTERY OF GODLINESS –

When JESUS was born as a human being through Mary at Bethlehem, He was still God, but had a human nature. He was 100 % fully God and 100 % fully human like us. As an eternal God, He cannot cease from being God. He took up humanity upon His divine nature. **Both natures, the divine and the human were blended in one person. This is the mystery of Godliness**. Nobody could comprehend (understand) how JESUS could be fully 100 % God and fully 100 % human at the same time.

Immanuel, God became human flesh (Matthew 1:21-23). Because JESUS became human flesh, He was the express image of God the Father. We can see God in the person of JESUS, and still not die. JESUS became the *visible Son of God* on earth for thirty-three and a half years.

5. JESUS CHRIST'S DIVINITY CANNOT BE BORN –

As an eternal God, JESUS was self-existent. He was **not** literally born in heaven. In heaven, JESUS was a self-existent God. Though He was a self-existent God, yet humbled Himself to take up the role of the Sin Bearer and to be called **"The Son of God."** (John 3:16). When He was born through Mary at Bethlehem, the plan of salvation fulfilled accordingly – (Isaiah 7:14; Matthew 1;21-23; Luke 1:35).

6. JESUS CHRIST'S HUMANITY WAS BORN THROUGH MARY AT BETHLEHEM –

JESUS WAS BORN ONCE AND DIED ONCE. HE WAS NOT BORN IN HEAVEN. HE WAS NOT BORN TWICE.

It was *the humanity* of JESUS that was born at Bethlehem. His **divinity** cannot be born nor can it be killed. Therefore, Mary gave birth ONLY to the **humanity** of JESUS. **She was the mother of JESUS CHRIST'S humanity. She was not the mother of God's divinity.**

God has no beginning; no mother and no father. Therefore, even though JESUS was a self-existent God, still Mary was **not** the mother of God. Remember Mary was pregnant by the Holy Spirit; not by Joseph.

Mary was another human being like us. She had a mother and a father. She was a sinner like us. **She ONLY gave birth to Jesus Christ's humanity at Bethlehem around 04 B.C.** (Matthew 1:21-23; Luke 1:31-35).

This is where JESUS is called – **"The Son of God."** Prior to the Incarnation, JESUS was an everlasting God in heaven and during the Old Testament time. Baby JESUS was the divine ONE; not Mary. We are to worship JESUS, not Mary.

7. JESUS CHRIST'S HUMANITY DIED AT CALARY.

When JESUS died at Calvary, it was His **humanity** that died. **His divinity cannot die**. And it was JESUS CHRIST'S **humanity** that got resurrected from the grave after three days. Remember? JESUS said, "Destroy this temple, and in three days I will raise it up." – (John 2:19).

8. AS GOD, JESUS DOES NOT NEED A GOD.

As a human being like us, He needs to pray to an eternal God for power. He was dependent upon the Father to be His God – (John 17:1-3). But as a self-existent God, He does not need God to help Him – (Matthew 4:4-7).

9. AS A HUMAN BEING, JESUS NEEDS TO PRAY TO GOD AS OUR EXAMPLE.

JESUS prayed to God the Father for help because as a human being, He needs a God. You can read the prayer of JESUS in John 17:1-3. That reveals that He was fully human like us.

Now, you should be able to understand what JESUS said in John 17:1-3 in His prayer to the Father at the Garden of Gethsemane before His arrest by the Roman soldiers on the night before His death on the Passover day (Friday), the 14 TH DAY OF THE MONTH OF NISAN (ABIB). Though JESUS was the God of Abraham and the children of Israel in the Old Testament, yet He acted as if He was not God. This is an act of humility, love, humbleness, meekness, and sacrifice for our sake.

This is the most amazing love story of all time. God the Creator became human flesh like us to save us from sin and eternal destruction, and give us eternal life.

....

THIS IS A DIAGRAM ABOUT THE TWO NATURES OF JESUS CHRIST.

NOTE: While JESUS was in human flesh for 33 and a half years on earth, HE had <u>two</u> natures in Him: the divine being and the human being were in one person.

Since JESUS was GOD before the incarnation, thus HE <u>did not</u> cease from being GOD. There was not a time that HE was not GOD.

Let's briefly look at the two natures in a diagram format to help our understanding much better of the GOD who became human flesh like us.

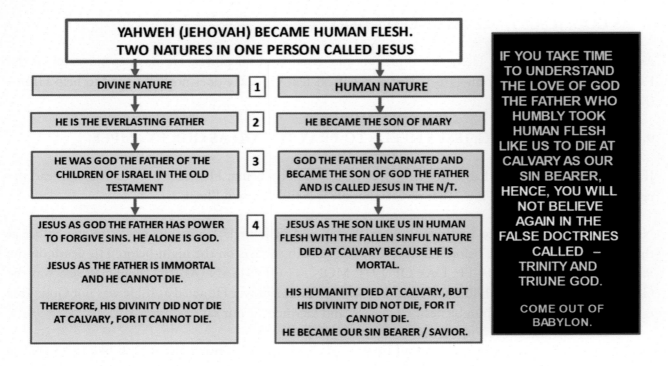

PRIOR TO THE INCARNATION THROUGH MARY AT BETHLEHEM AROUND 04 B.C., JESUS WAS THE YAHWEH (JEHOVAH) WHO SPOKE TO PROPHET ISAIAH.

THE GOD WHO SPOKE TO PROPHET ISAIAH IS THE ONLY ONE GOD IN HEAVEN.   HE IS JESUS!

- Isaiah 43:10
- 10 Ye are my witnesses, saith the   LORD, and my servant whom I have chosen: that ye may know and believe me, and understand   that I am he: before me there was no God formed, neither shall there be after me.

THE REDEEMER

- Isaiah 44:6
- 6 Thus saith the LORD the King of Israel, and his redeemer   the LORD of hosts; I am the first, and I am the last; and   beside me there is no God   .

THE CREATOR

- Isaiah 44:24
- 24 Thus saith the   LORD, thy redeemer , and he that formed thee from the womb   , I am the LORD that maketh all things; that stretcheth   forth the heavens   alone; that spreadeth   abroad the earth by   myself;

THE PROPHECY OF HIS DEATH AT CALVARY

- Isaiah 49:16
- 16 Behold, I have graven thee upon the palms of my hands   ; thy walls are continually before me.

SO, WHEN YAHWEH (JEHOVAH) BECAME HUMAN FLESH, HE DID NOT CEASE FROM BEING GOD. HE HUMBLY BECAME THE SON OF GOD, YET STILL GOD THE FATHER. TWO NATURES IN HIM WHILE IN HUMAN FLESH.

CHAPTER 15

UNDERSTANDING THE TRUTH – FIRST THINGS FIRST.

Scripture:

Genesis 1:1 – In the beginning God (Elohim) created the heaven and the earth - (KJV).

The text above (Genesis 1:1) is the **main key text** for those of us who professed to believe in JESUS as our Savior and in the Bible as the only rule of faith (Sola Scriptura). The Bible which is the word of God begins by introducing **GOD (ELOHIM)** as the Creator of heaven and earth.

We must analyze this text above in the context of the whole Bible in relation the **sayings** of JESUS while he was on earth with the disciples as recorded in the four gospels – Matthew, Mark, Luke, and John.

The first thing for us as professed Christians is to take time to learn and understand the GOD (ELOHIM / YAHWEH) which is introduced as the Creator in Genesis 1:1-31.

We must ask the crucial question: Who is ELOHIM which is JEHOVAH (YAHWEH) introduced as the Creator in Genesis 1:1? The Bible introduced GOD (ELOHIM / YAHWEH / JEHOVAH) as the Creator.

Let's be clear from here. The Bible did <u>not</u> introduce <u>the Son of GOD as the Creator</u>. There was <u>no</u> Son of GOD that existed in heaven *before* the angels existed.

Let me reiterate the point again in simple language so that you don't miss it.

There was <u>no</u> Son of GOD that existed in heaven when our planet earth was created as recorded in Genesis 1:1-31.

If we failed to learn and understand this fundamental truth stated above, then we are deceived and very behind since we are in the 21ST century (A.D.).

....

Understanding that JESUS was YAHWEH (JEHOVAH), the Almighty GOD of Abraham, Isaac, and Jacob who created heaven and earth is so important for us to know because he did not create one baby sinner to this earth after Adam and Eve's fall. No baby inherited the sins of Adam and Eve.

YAHWEH (JEHOVAH) did not have a Son called JESUS in heaven before the angels existed. Why? Because JESUS was the ELOHIM (YAHWEH / JEHOVAH) who created the angels in heaven *before* he created our planet earth.

THE HEBREW TEXT OF GENESIS 1:1

- In the Masoretic Text the verse is as follows in seven words:
- בְּרֵאשִׁית בָּרָא אֱלֹהִים אֵת הַשָּׁמַיִם וְאֵת הָאָרֶץ

ELOHIM

- **The same HEBREW word   (Elohim) is used in Genesis 1:1 , 3, 26 , 27 , 31 , 2:1 -3; and Exodus 20:1 -3.**
- **In English, "ELOHIM " is called   – "GOD. "**
- **HE IS THE LORD OF THE SABBATH named JESUS who created heaven and earth.**
- **(Mark 2:28 ; John 1:1 -3, 14 ; 5:39 , 46 ; 8:58).**

JESUS was the everlasting Father of the children of Israel in the OLD TESTAMENT who humbly incarnated into human flesh through Mary at Bethlehem and became the Son of God. (Did you get that or no?).

....

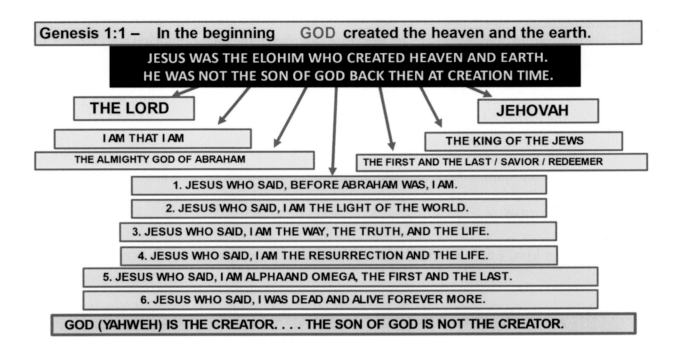

Genesis 1:1 – In the beginning GOD created the heaven and the earth.

JESUS WAS THE ELOHIM WHO CREATED HEAVEN AND EARTH.
HE WAS NOT THE SON OF GOD BACK THEN AT CREATION TIME.

THE LORD

JEHOVAH

I AM THAT I AM

THE KING OF THE JEWS

THE ALMIGHTY GOD OF ABRAHAM

THE FIRST AND THE LAST / SAVIOR / REDEEMER

1. JESUS WHO SAID, BEFORE ABRAHAM WAS, I AM.

2. JESUS WHO SAID, I AM THE LIGHT OF THE WORLD.

3. JESUS WHO SAID, I AM THE WAY, THE TRUTH, AND THE LIFE.

4. JESUS WHO SAID, I AM THE RESURRECTION AND THE LIFE.

5. JESUS WHO SAID, I AM ALPHA AND OMEGA, THE FIRST AND THE LAST.

6. JESUS WHO SAID, I WAS DEAD AND ALIVE FOREVER MORE.

GOD (YAHWEH) IS THE CREATOR. . . . THE SON OF GOD IS NOT THE CREATOR.

- **JESUS was the everlasting Father of the children of Israel in the OLD TESTAMENT who <u>humbly incarnated</u> into human flesh through Mary at Bethlehem and became the Son of God.**

- Isaiah 7:14; 9:6; 44:6, 24; 49:16; Matthew 1:21 -23; Luke 1:35.

It was only at Bethlehem through Mary around 04 B.C., that <u>ELOHIM (YAHWEH / JEHOVAH) became human flesh and is called JESUS, the Son of God</u>. It was <u>**NOT**</u> the Son of God that became human flesh at Bethlehem. (Isaiah 7:14; 9:6; 44:6, 24; 49:16; Matthew 1:21-23; Luke 1:35).

While *in human flesh* for thirty-three and a half years on earth as God's Son, JESUS was still the everlasting Father in heaven, but in Spirit form. He did **not** cease from being the everlasting God the Father while in human flesh on earth. He had two natures.

In human flesh, JESUS was the visible image of GOD the Father. He said to Phillip, **when you see me, you have seen the Father** – (**John 14:6-9**). He also said, "I and the Father are one." IMMANUEL became human flesh and dwelt among men on earth.

....

Scripture: John 14:6-9

⁶Jesus saith unto him, I am the way, the truth, and the life: no man cometh unto the Father, but by me.

⁷If ye had known me, ye should have known my Father also: and from henceforth ye know him, and have seen him.

⁸Philip saith unto him, Lord, show us the Father, and it sufficeth us.

⁹Jesus saith unto him, Have I been so long time with you, and yet hast thou not known me, Philip? he that hath seen me hath seen the Father; and how sayest thou then, Show us the Father?

....

JESUS IS THE FATHER WHO CAME IN HUMAN FLESH TO DWELL AMONGST MEN.

JESUS IS THE FATHER

- John 14:6 -9
- ⁶Jesus saith unto him, I am the way, the truth, and the life: no man cometh unto the Father, but by me.

- ⁷ If ye had known me, ye should have known my Father also: and from henceforth ye know him, and have seen him.

- ⁸ Philip saith unto him, Lord, show us the Father, and it sufficeth us .
- ⁹ Jesus saith unto him, Have I been so long time with you, and yet hast thou not known me, Philip? he that hath seen me hath seen the Father ; and how sayest thou then, Show us the Father?

....

THE GOD WHO CREATED THE LIGHT, CREATED <u>NO</u> BABY SINNERS FROM ADAM.

....

WHO WAS THIS GOD (YAHWEH) WHO CREATED THE LIGHT?

He was the Almighty GOD of Abraham, Isaac, and Jacob who became human flesh through Mary at Bethlehem. <u>His name is JESUS</u> – (Matthew 1:21-23; Luke 1:35).

In the Old Testament, He was the JEHOVAH of the children of Israel who delivered them from slavery in Egypt. He alone created heaven and earth in six literal days (Genesis 1:31; 2:1-3). He spoke to Moses at the burning bush, as recorded in Exodus 3:13-14.

....

THE GOD (YAHWEH) WHO CREATED THE LIGHT.

Who? Jesus. Read   - Genesis 1:1 -3; John 5:39, 46; 8:12   , 56 -58 .

JESUS WAS THE ALMIGHTY GOD OF ABRAHAM CALLED – "I AM THAT I AM," "JEHOVAH," AND "THE FIRST AND THE LAST"– Exodus 3:6, 13-14; Exodus 6:1-3; Isaiah 26:4; 44:6, 24; 49:16; John 8:56-58; Revelation 1:17-18; 21:6-7.

///

FOUR INNOCENT BABIES / CHILDREN – CREATED BY A LOVING GOD.

GOD CREATED **NO** BABY SINNERS FROM ADAM.

THESE FOUR CHILDREN ARE SO INNOCENT AND KNOW NOTHING ABOUT SIN.

SATAN IS THE LIAR IN MAKING PEOPLE TO BELIEVE THAT BABIES ARE BORN SINNERS DUE TO ADAM'S SIN.

THE DEVIL MADE PEOPLE TO BELIEVE THAT "SIN IS INHERITED FROM ADAM."

GOD LOVED US AND HE WOULD NOT CREATE ANY BABY IN THE DEVIL'S IMAGE, A SINNER, A MURDERER, A PROSTITUTE, AN ADULTERER, A ROBBER.

THE DIFFERENCE BETWEEN THE FIRST DEATH AND THE SECOND DEATH (ETERNAL DEATH).

- Again, the timeline chart below will show you clearly that God created no baby sinners from Adam. And the *first* death is **not** the evidence that a baby is born a sinner since *we all inherited the first death* from Adam. No one inherited *the second death* (eternal death) from Adam.

- The *second* death is a choice. And it is the wages (PENALTY) of sin for the individual person. You only become a sinner when you transgress God's law; **not** when you die the first death.

1. No person is a sinner by Adam's sin.
2. No person is a sinner by being born with the fallen sinful nature.
3. No person is a sinner by dying the first death during his or her lifetime.
4. No person inherited sin from Adam.
5. No person inherited the second death (eternal death) from Adam.
6. The second death is the wages (penalty) of sin by an individual who chooses to transgress God's law and repent not.
7. The first death is not the evidence that one is born a sinner.
8. We all inherited the first death from Adam, and the first death is only a temporary sleep; not the death of a sinner– (Romans 5:12).
9. When you transgress God's law, that is the time you become a sinner and in need of a Savior.
10. You are in need of a Savior / Sin Bearer when you transgress God's LAW – (1 John 3:4).

Author: Metusela F. Albert

CHAPTER 16

THE MISINTERPRETED SCRIPTURE – PSALM 51:5

Scripture:

Psalm 51:1-5 (KJV)

1. Have mercy upon me, <u>O God</u>, according to thy lovingkindness: according unto the multitude of thy tender mercies blot out my transgressions.

² Wash me throughly from mine iniquity, and cleanse me from my sin.

³ <u>For I acknowledge my transgressions: and my sin is ever before me</u>.

⁴ Against thee, thee only, have I sinned, and done this evil in thy sight: that thou mightest be justified when thou speakest, and be clear when thou judgest.

⁵ Behold, I was shapen in iniquity; and in sin did my mother conceive me.

....

EXPLANATION

You cannot interpret Scripture to contradict who GOD is. And you cannot interpret Scripture to contradict another doctrine in the same Bible. Furthermore, common sense will tell you that you cannot interpret Scripture to imply that it was GOD who created baby sinners, killers, adulterers, idol worshippers, from Adam's sin. Think folks. Think! Think!

Always read the Bible in the context of who GOD is. This is rule # 1 when you become a Bible student. Therefore, Psalm 51:5 must be read in <u>the context of who God is</u> and also in <u>the context of David's confession and repentance</u>. IF you ignored these principles of interpretation, then you will find yourself contradicting Scripture and God who created us in his own image.

Another rule of interpretation is – Allow Scripture to interpret itself (precept upon precept) in a Chronological Order.

The event in 2 Samuel Chapter 11 took place first. It was the sin called *adultery* and *murder* that led David to genuinely confess and repent in Psalm 51:1-5. Surely, David was not confessing and repenting because of his fallen sinful nature. Surely, David was not excusing his sins. He admitted his sins and genuinely confessed and repented. Read the context in a Chronological order.

Did you realize it? GOD used prophet Nathan to confront David in 2 Samuel Chapter 12.

LET'S GET THIS CORRECT FROM TODAY SO THAT YOU STOP MISINTERPRETING PSALM 51:5.

1. David did **not** commit adultery and murder because of his fallen sinful nature.

2. David did **not** transgress the law on adultery and murder because of Adam's sin.

3. David did **not** inherit Adam's sin.

4. David did **not** confess and repent in Psalm 51:1-4 because of his fallen sinful nature inherited from Adam.

5. David was **not** born a sinner, nor an adulterer, nor a murderer because of Adam's sin.

6. David and Bathsheba were the adulterers in 2 Samuel Chapter 11.

7. The fallen sinful nature does **not** make one baby a sinner in the mother's womb.

8. Sin has to do with the transgression of GOD'S law – (1 John 3:4).

9. David transgressed the law on adultery with Bathsheba because of his own choice to fulfill his own LUST (evil desire).

10. David transgressed the law on murder of Uriah to cover up his sin of adultery with Bathsheba. But GOD saw it. And no sin can be excused nor hide from GOD.

11. Whosoever transgresseth the law is of the devil. (1 John 3:7-9).

12. When David transgressed the law on adultery and murder, he was no longer the man after God's heart, until his *genuine* confession and repentance. Relationship with God is restored when there is *genuine* confession and repentance from sin – (Psalm 51:1-4).

13. IF there is NO *genuine* confession and repentance, there is no forgiveness and assurance of salvation from GOD. (NOTE: Achan who took the wealth in Jericho repented because of the fear of the consequences after he was found to be the cause of their defeat by the little town of AI, thus his repentance was not genuine).

LET ME SOUND THE WARNING TO ALL PASTORS AND CHURCH LEADERS IN A DENOMINATION.

IF you have been believing a lie for a long time, then Common Sense in you is what God uses to tell you that you are contradicting the Scriptures after the truth is presented in a clear way, and the error is exposed. That is the work of the Holy Spirit in arousing your mind to the truth against the error. Common sense and logic thinking play an important part. This is sound reasoning and thinking logically.

But if you ignored and rejected the truth, then you are sinning against the Holy Spirit, and the error will blind you further and you will continue to believe a lie, thinking that it is the truth.

God will send you a delusion to believe a lie because you refused to believe the truth which proves you loved the error from Satan more than JESUS, your Creator and Savior – (2 Thessalonians 2:9-11).

Many Pastors and Church leaders who work for a Mainline Denomination ignored and reject the truth when they chose to believe what their Denomination teaches which is false because of many factors, as listed below.

1. **They chose to have power in the Church.**

2. **They chose fame among the people in the Denomination.**

3. **They chose to receive their pay check from the Denomination.**

4. **They chose to believe that their Church cannot be wrong since their Church is God's remnant Church.**

5. **They chose to believe that their Church has an appointed prophet called by God and he or she is the reason their Church existed after 1798 A.D.**

6. **They chose to receive their pension from the Church after retirement.**

7. **They chose not to lose their position of power in the Church.**

Are you one that is reading this book and have become convicted by the Holy Spirit that Babies Are NOT Born Sinners from Adam's sin? . . . Well, tell the truth in your congregation and admit to them that your Denomination is wrong in regard to this evil doctrine. Take a strong stand on JESUS against evil doctrines that make JESUS the creator of baby sinners.

He or she who loves his or her Church more than JESUS is not worthy of Him. Please reject your Church's false teaching and accept JESUS and his truth. . . .

Don't be afraid of those who can kill the body, but be afraid of the One who can kill your body and your soul in hell – (Matthew 10:27).

Of course, JESUS who was YAHWEH (JEHOVAH) in the Old Testament who created heaven and earth, created no baby sinners from Adam. Amen! Amen! Amen!

PONT # 1: INTERPRET SCRIPTURE IN THE CONTEXT OF WHO GOD IS –

1. GOD is love – (1 John 4:8).

2. GOD created us in his image – (Genesis 1:27; 5:1-4).

3. GOD created not one baby in the image of the devil, a sinner, a liar, a murderer – (John 8:44).

4. GOD who loved us gave himself to become a human being like us to enable him to die at Calvary as our Sin Bearer / Savior - (Matthew 1:21-23; Luke 1:35).

5. GOD who made us is returning again to take his saints to heaven – (1 Thessalonians 4:16-17; Revelation 1:7)

PONT # 2: INTERPRET SCRIPTURE IN THE CONTEXT OF DAVID'S CONFESSION AND REPENTANCE.

1. GOD created all human beings from Adam and Eve.

2. We as human beings are all descendants of Adam and Eve.

3. GOD created us in his own image.

4. GOD did not create one baby in the image of the devil.

5. GOD created no baby sinner from Adam's sin nor in the devil's image.

POINT # 3: INTERPRET SCRIPTURE IN THE CONTEXT OF CHRONOLOGICAL ORDER

For example, Psalm 51 is the confession and repentance of David's sin recorded in 2 Samuel Chapter 11:1-27. David's sin of adultery with Bathsheba, followed by the murder of Uriah, the husband of Bathsheba, was planned to cover up his iniquity. Though he tried to cover up the pregnancy of Bathsheba from the eyes of the people while Uriah was out in war, but he cannot hide it from GOD.

GOD revealed the iniquity of King David to Prophet Nathan who confronted him – (2 Samuel Chapter 12). And in Psalm 51:1-5, David came openly to confess and repent of his sins. He admitted it. That is a record of David's genuine confession and repentance written as a lesson for future generations.

Unfortunately, our generation today misinterpreted David's prayer in Psalm 51:5 to excuse sin by telling us that David was born a sinner. Sadly, they are telling us that David committed adultery and murder because God created him a sinner, an adulterer, a murderer. This is a Satanic evil interpretation that we must confront, rebuke, and condemn.

POINT # 4: INTERPRET SCRIPTURE IN THE CONTEXT OF GOD'S PLAN OF SALVATION FOR MANKIND AND THE DESTRUCTION OF SATAN AND HIS FOLLOWERS.

The Timeline Chart Below Showing the First and Second Resurrections and the Destruction of Satan at the end of the Millennium is a must for Bible Students and Scholars to Keep in Mind the GREAT PLAN OF GOD to understand subjects like – Sin and Salvation.

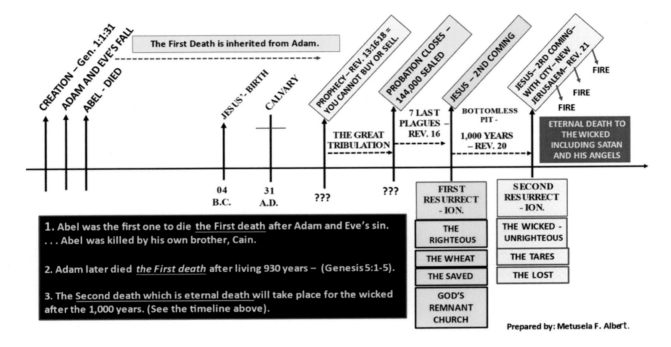

1. Abel was the first one to die the First death after Adam and Eve's sin. . . . Abel was killed by his own brother, Cain.

2. Adam later died *the First death* after living 930 years – (Genesis 5:1-5).

3. The Second death which is eternal death will take place for the wicked after the 1,000 years. (See the timeline above).

Prepared by: Metusela F. Albert.

CHAPTER 17

HOW DO WE INTERPRET ROMANS 3:23?

SCRIPTURE:

Romans 3:23 -

²³ For <u>all</u> have sinned, and come short of the glory of God;

....

EXPLANATION

An elementary student of the Bible will always ignore the principles of interpretation and take that Scripture to mean that the word "all" in the text, means – the <u>baby in the mother's womb at conception is a sinner</u>.

Since most people have already believed that the fallen sinful in itself is sin, therefore, the Churches and the Pastors believed that Romans 3:23 is the Bible text to support their doctrine of Babies are born sinners. Sad to say, they failed to do a correct interpretation of the text.

They have implied that God who created us made baby sinners from Adam. That is a devilish interpretation of Scripture.

....

PLEASE LISTEN CAREFULLY SO THAT YOU STOP MAKING GOD AS THE CREATOR OF BABY SINNERS.

1. When Paul wrote that letter to the Church members in Roman, he was addressing the issue of sin with the church members who could understand his letter; not with the baby in a mother's womb in Church.

2. Paul was talking in his letter to those in the Church in Rome who can understand him. Remember, a three month old baby in the church cannot understand his letter and the issues raised, let alone a baby in the mother's womb.

3. When Paul said, "All have sinned and come short of the glory of God," that he meant "All" who heard and understood him.

4. None who understood Paul's letter can deny that he or she has not sinned.

5. I can say the same thing to anyone who is reading this book – "All of us have sinned and come short of the glory of God." I did not mean the babies.

Dear folks, please use common sense and logic thinking to reason when we read the Scriptures. Avoid misinterpreting Scripture to contradict God's word. Stop making God to become the Creator of baby sinners, murderers, adulterers, prostitutes, fornicators, robbers, idol worshippers, drug addicts, drunkards, etc.

....

- The death of JESUS at Calvary as our Sin Bearer proves that NO BABY was ever born with Adam and Eve's sins.
- IF the sins of Adam and Eve were inherited by all babies beginning with Cain and Abel, then Babies would have become the Sin Bearer for Adam and Eve.
- And the gospel becomes distorted, null, and void.

CHAPTER 18

THE THEOLOGY OF THE PHARISEES INFECTED TODAY'S CHURCHES.

Scripture:

John 9:1-10

1. And as <u>Jesus</u> passed by, <u>he saw a man which was blind from his birth</u>.

² And his disciples asked him, saying, Master, <u>who did sin, this man, or his parents, that he was born blind?</u>

³ Jesus answered, <u>Neither hath this man sinned, nor his parents: but that the works of God should be made manifest in him.</u>

⁴ I must work the works of him that sent me, while it is day: the night cometh, when no man can work.

⁵ <u>As long as I am in the world, I am the light of the world.</u>

⁶ When he had thus spoken, <u>he spat on the ground, and made clay of the spittle, and he anointed the eyes of the blind man with the clay,</u>

⁷ And said unto him, <u>Go, wash in the pool of Siloam, (which is by interpretation, Sent.) He went his way therefore, and washed, and came seeing.</u>

⁸ The neighbours therefore, and they which before had seen him that he was blind, said, Is not this he that sat and begged?

⁹ Some said, This is he: others said, He is like him: <u>but he said, I am he</u>.

¹⁰ Therefore said they unto him, How were thine eyes opened?

¹¹ <u>He answered and said, A man that is called Jesus made clay, and anointed mine eyes, and said unto me, Go to the pool of Siloam, and wash: and I went and washed, and I received sight.</u>

[12] Then said they unto him, Where is he? He said, I know not.

[13] They brought to the Pharisees him that aforetime was blind.

[14] **And it was the sabbath day when Jesus made the clay, and opened his eyes.**

[15] Then again the Pharisees also asked him how he had received his sight. He said unto them, **He put clay upon mine eyes, and I washed, and do see.**

[21] **But by what means he now seeth, we know not; or who hath opened his eyes, we know not: he is of age; ask him: he shall speak for himself.**

[22] **These words spake his parents, because they feared the Jews: for the Jews had agreed already, that if any man did confess that he was Christ, he should be put out of the synagogue.**

[23] **Therefore said his parents, He is of age; ask him.**

[24] **Then again called they the man that was blind, and said unto him, Give God the praise: we know that this man is a sinner.**

[25] **He answered and said, Whether he be a sinner or no, I know not: one thing I know, that, whereas I was blind, now I see.**

[26] **Then said they to him again, What did he to thee? how opened he thine eyes?**

[27] **He answered them, I have told you already, and ye did not hear: wherefore would ye hear it again? will ye also be his disciples?**

[28] **Then they reviled him, and said, Thou art his disciple; but we are Moses' disciples.**

[29] **We know that God spake unto Moses: as for this fellow, we know not from whence he is.**

[30] **The man answered and said unto them, Why herein is a marvellous thing, that ye know not from whence he is, and yet he hath opened mine eyes.**

[31] **Now we know that God heareth not sinners: but if any man be a worshipper of God, and doeth his will, him he heareth.**

[32] **Since the world began was it not heard that any man opened the eyes of one that was born blind.**

[33] **If this man were not of God, he could do nothing.**

[34] **They answered and said unto him, Thou wast altogether born in sins, and dost thou teach us? And they cast him out.**

³⁵ Jesus heard that they had cast him out; and when he had found him, he said unto him, Dost thou believe on the Son of God?

³⁶ He answered and said, Who is he, Lord, that I might believe on him?

³⁷ And Jesus said unto him, Thou hast both seen him, and it is he that talketh with thee.

³⁸ And he said, Lord, I believe. And he worshipped him.

³⁹ And Jesus said, For judgment I am come into this world, that they which see not might see; and that they which see might be made blind.

⁴⁰ And some of the Pharisees which were with him heard these words, and said unto him, Are we blind also?

⁴¹ Jesus said unto them, If ye were blind, ye should have no sin: but now ye say, We see; therefore your sin remaineth.

....

EXPLANATION

1. The Pharisees believed that the man born blind was born a sinner – (John 9:34).

2. But JESUS made it clear that the man born blind was not a sinner by birth.

....

Unfortunately, there are many who can see but they are blind, just like those Pharisees.

Being blind does not necessarily mean you were born a sinner. One can be born crippled, but not born a sinner; for sin is by the transgression of God's law.

We really need to condemn that false theology that says, We are born sinners due to Adam's sin we inherited.

In fact, that theology should have no place in the Christian Church because it makes Christianity a mockery. It immortalizes and excuses sin in every generation. What a shame!

....

CHAPTER 19

THE ORIGINAL SIN CONCEPT BY THE CATHOLIC CHURCH.

The Catholic Church teaching of original sin says, the fallen sinful nature is sin in itself. As a result, they created another doctrine to make JESUS not become a natural sinner. They came up with the doctrine called – IMMACULATE CONCEPTION OF MARY. What does it mean?

It means, she is a sinless virgin Mary who gave birth to JESUS and he was not born with the fallen sinful nature like us to avoid being a sinner. Therefore, according to the Catholic Church, we are all born sinners except for JESUS who was born of Mary. They believed that Mary was the mother of God since JESUS is God – God the Son. They also believed that the Holy Spirit is God – God the Holy Spirit. They came up with the Trinity doctrine of God the Father, God the Son, and God the Holy Spirit.

They came up with another doctrine called – <u>infant baptism</u> since they believed that the baby is born a sinner due to the fallen sinful nature.

The POTESTANT CHURCHES came out of the Catholic Church, the Lutheran Church is the first. And they took the Catholic Church belief on ORIGINAL SIN which says, the fallen Sinful nature is sin in itself and Babies are born sinners.

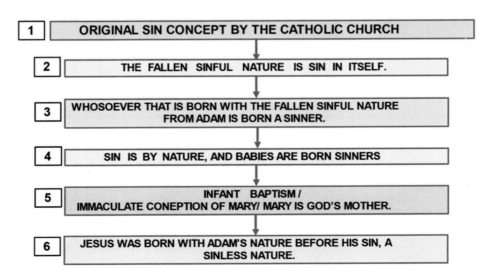

1. ORIGINAL SIN CONCEPT BY THE CATHOLIC CHURCH

2. THE FALLEN SINFUL NATURE IS SIN IN ITSELF.

3. WHOSOEVER THAT IS BORN WITH THE FALLEN SINFUL NATURE FROM ADAM IS BORN A SINNER.

4. SIN IS BY NATURE, AND BABIES ARE BORN SINNERS

5. INFANT BAPTISM / IMMACULATE CONEPTION OF MARY/ MARY IS GOD'S MOTHER.

6. JESUS WAS BORN WITH ADAM'S NATURE BEFORE HIS SIN, A SINLESS NATURE.

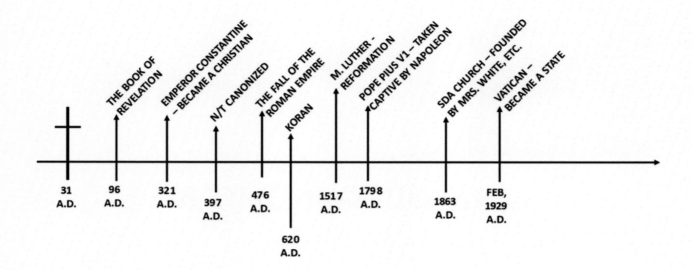

THE CATHOLIC CHURCH DOCTRINE OF BABIES ARE BORN SINNERS
PERMEATED THE PROTESTANT CHURCHES

- **ARE YOU "IN NEED OF A GOD" OR "IN NEED OF A SAVIOR".**
- From the time of your birth, you need a   God to keep your alive. You don't need a Savior while in your mother's womb because you are not a sinner. You have no sins to be forgiven as a baby.   No sins to confess and repent from.
- From the time you transgressed   God's law and became a sinner at the age of accountability, that is the time you need a Savior. Only the blood of the Savior can cleanse your sins. Without the blood of JESUS, there is no remission of sins.
- Needing God and needing a Savior are two different things.
- NOTE: JESUS who did not sin at all, only needs a God to help him overcome temptations   – (John 17:1 -3). He did not need a Savior because he did not sin.
- Had JESUS transgressed the law when he was tempted as we are (Hebrews 4:15), then he would require a Savior, and the world would be lost since he failed and none can become our Savior. Of course, no one could replace him.
- Thank you JESUS for being our God and Savior also. You alone are God. You are our Creator, the Almighty God of Abraham, Isaac, and Jacob who humbly became human flesh through Mary at Bethlehem to die at Calvary as our Sin Bearer.

- Written by the Author of the Book   – "God Created No Baby Sinners From Adam."   Metusela F. Albert.

CHAPTER 20

SIN IS IMMORTALIZED BY THE CHURCH.

Many people don't realize that when their Church (denomination) teaches "Babies are born sinners due to Adam's sin" and "Sin is by nature," hence it is their Church that is corrupt. It is their Church that teaches the people to continue living in sin.

And their Church is selling a doctrine that indirectly says, God created all babies to be sinners due Adam's sin. In fact, their Church has immortalized sin and gave the members a life time excuse to sin believing that they can be saved "in" sin. Actually, JESUS did <u>not</u> come to save us in sin, but "FROM" sin. (Matthew 1:21-23).

The "Sin Theory" that says, "The fallen sinful nature is equal to sin; therefore, sin is by nature," is the <u>*root*</u> problem. This is the false doctrine that needs to be condemned and uprooted from the Churches, mainline denominations, Pastors, and believers in Jesus that called themselves - Christians.

Why? Because this doctrine immortalizes sin in all babies, beginning from the first baby born to this earth which is Cain, and goes to the last baby before Jesus returns. In other words, they are telling us that Cain killed his brother Abel because Cain was born a killer (a sinner) due to the sins of his parents, Adam and Eve.

That kind of theology (sin theory) has no place in the Christian Church. Sadly, the Churches are so corrupt that they cannot see the heresy of such teaching. Adultery is so prevalent in the Churches of today because the Church tells them they were born Adulterers from Adam's Sin. They blamed God for creating them that way. They excused their adulterous acts by blaming on Adam's sin as the cause of their evil actions. And Satan blinded them from not seeing the evil teachings.

IT IS THE CHURCH THAT PROMOTES SIN DUE TO ITS FALSE TEACHINGS, AS LISTED BELOW:

1. The fallen sinful nature is sin in itself.

2. Since we are born with the fallen sinful nature inherited from Adam, therefore, we are born sinners at conception time in the mother's womb.

3. Sin is by nature.

4. Sin is by birth.

5. Sin is inherited.

6. Sin is without one's choice.

7. Sin is a state.

8. Sin is a condition.

9. Sin is what we are.

10. We are sinners by what we are.

11. Sin is universal due to Adam's sin in us.

12. In order to be a sinner, all one has to do is to be born.

13. <u>Sin is universal</u> without your choice, therefore, <u>Salvation is also universal</u>

(unconditional) without your choice.

14. We will continue to sin till death because of the fallen sinful nature in us, and we will be saved in sin.

15. Your sins – past, present, and future were already forgiven at Calvary. The sins you have not committed yet, we forgiven already in advance without your confession and repentance.

16. The reason we confess and repent of our sins is because we have already been forgiven and given the gift of eternal life at Calvary unconditionally.

....

DID YOU REALIZE THE EVILNESS OF THOSE 16 DOCTRINES LISTED ABOVE?

THOSE ARE 16 SATANIC DOCTRINES CAUSED BY THE ONE EVIL DOCTRINE CALLED – THE FALLEN SINFUL NATURE IS SIN IN ITSELF.

When you know the truth, you will easily know the error(s). But if you don't know the truth, you will not know the error(s).

Why not help your friends and other pastors to learn of the truth? Let's share the truth more aggressively that the world may be cured from this PANDEMIC in the Churches.

Give God the glory.

....

CONCLUSION

The belief that says, "All babies are born sinners due to Adam's sin in us," has been proven wrong. Professed Christians should not believe again in such false doctrine that makes the death of JESUS null and void.

If you have not understood it yet after reading this book, then pray earnestly for JESUS to appear to you on your road to Damascus as he did to Paul.

May God bless your heart and give you good health and wealth to share the truth in your Ministry to expand God's kingdom and his truth.

Don't ever forget this: God who created us in his image made no baby sinners from Adam's sin.

Satan is the liar who tries to distort the gospel in different ways. He is trying to misinterpret Scripture in a subtle way to make the gospel null and void. But you who can think and reason logically do not have to believe again in the devil's lies from today. Give God the glory and praise the name of JESUS. Amen! Amen! And Amen!

//

THE SATANIC ATTACK UPON THE GOSPEL

- IF Adam and Eve's sins were transferred to _all babies AND babies became sinners due to Adam and Eve's sins_, then babies would have become Adam and Eve's Sin Bearer. And the gospel where JESUS alone is the Sin Bearer for all mankind including Adam and Eve would have become null and void.

- Therefore, the death of JESUS at Calvary would mean nothing.

- Don't the Pastors, Churches, and Mainline Denominations of the 21st century (A.D.) realize how evil is their doctrine called "Babies Are Born Sinners due to Adam's sin" ??????

- . . . .

- IF sin is by nature due to Adam's sin that we inherited without a choice, then sin is immortalized by the churches that advocated this evil doctrine. And expect sin to prevail in the churches because sin is excusable.

- Indirectly, God is now the Creator of Baby sinners in the devil's image.

- Therefore, the death of JESUS at Calvary would mean nothing.

- Don't the Pastors, Churches, and Mainline Denominations of the 21st century (A.D.) realize how evil is their doctrine called "Babies Are Born Sinners due to Adam's sin" AND "Sin is by nature." ??????

- ....

Prepared by: Metusela F. Albert

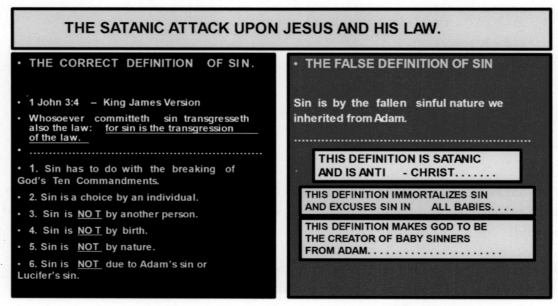

Prepared by: Metusela F. Albert

MY STORY

In 1972, at the age of 19 years, I became a baptized member of the Seventh-day Adventist Church in Fiji and Rotuma which is part of the world-wide Church. And in 1986, I decided to join the Ministry. In1994, I became an ordained Pastor of the SDA Church. Though the SDA Church believed and advocated the false doctrine that says "Babies are born sinners due to Adam's sin in us by inheritance," I did not believe what the Church believes regarding this subject. To me, it is an evil doctrine.

I continued to teach and preach that sin is the transgression of God's law, and we are not born sinners, while working as a Pastor in the SDA Church in Fiji. My intention was to make as many people to believe the truth in the Bible; not in the Church's Fundamental Beliefs and false teachings.

I knew that one day I might be disciplined by the Church leaders for not believing the Fundamental Beliefs of the SDA Church. However, that did not bother me. Believing in JESUS who created us in his image, as sinless babies, is more important than teaching the error of the Church.

While in the SDA Church, I openly stated my disapproval of such a doctrine and many Colleagues of mine opposed it and called me heretical. So sad that they did not know what I knew on this subject. They were the majority, but that did not weaken my faith in JESUS and the truth. Remember, the majority were drowned by the flood during Noah's time. Only 8 people were inside the Ark. When it comes to the truth in God's eyes, it is not measured by the quantity. Truth is always the truth because God says it; not what the denomination or the church says it. Don't miss this. Peter and the disciples said, we ought to obey God rather than men – (Acts 5:29).

In 2006 came my separation from the SDA Church. No regrets when truth is above the error. Some people knew the truth, but they compromised for their own personal gain and went against God.

In 2011, I wrote my first book – "15 Reasons Why Babies Aren't Born Sinners."

Ten years later (May 2021), I decided to write and publish this book – "God Created No Baby Sinners from Adam."

I gave a title that perhaps may capture the attention of the readers to re-think of their God who created all babies in his image. We were all created in God's image; not in the devil's image. That is the strong point to convince anyone with a sound mind.

Why should a loving God create baby sinners in the image of the devil? Think folks. Think! Think! Think!

As a Preacher of the gospel, I am a teacher also and I have to find ways to capture the attention of the listeners to hear the point I wanted to get across. I have to be more aggressive in taking the truth. And the truth must be written for the generations to come. That is why I wrote this Book and created the Chapters to catch the readers' attention to wake them up from the false teachings in the Churches.

This is a serious subject. What a man thinketh in his heart, so is he. What you believed will affect your lifestyle, and also your character and destiny.

IF someone believes that he or she is a sinner, a murderer, a prostitute, an adulterer, a child molester, a drug addict, a drunkard, an idol worshipper, because it was God who created him or her that way due to Adam's sin in us by inheritance, then that person has an excuse to sin, to kill, to molest children, to do whatever, and believe also that God will save him unconditionally because it was God who made him a natural sinner. This kind of theology is excusing and immortalizing sin in the churches, in the community, in the society, in the nation. It is the church that teaches people to kill, steal, commit adultery, worship idols, etc. That is a doctrine of a corrupt church. Did I say, a corrupt Church? Of course!

REMEMBER THIS:

1. GOD CREATED NOT EVEN ONE BABY SINNER TO THIS EARTH.

2. ADAM'S SIN IS NOT THE CAUSE FOR YOU TO COMMIT SIN.

3. NO BABY IS THE SIN BEARER FOR ADAM. THAT IS THE REASON, NO BABY IS BORN A SINNER BY ADAM'S SIN.

4. JESUS TOOK THE FALLEN SINFUL NATURE OF ADAM THROUGH MARY AND HE WAS NOT A SINNER BY NATURE, THEREFORE, NO BABY THAT IS BORN WITH THE FALLEN SINFUL NATURE IS A NATURAL SINNER.

5. SIN CANNOT BE INHERITED BECAUSE <u>JESUS IS THE SIN BEARER</u> AND ALL SIN IS TRANSFERRED TO JESUS.

6. YOU ARE A SINNER IN NEED OF A SAVIOR (JESUS) BECAUSE YOU TRANSGRESSED GOD'S LAW FROM THE AGE OF ACCOUNTABILITY.

7. YOU ARE NOT IN NEED OF A SAVIOR BECAUSE YOU HAVE A SINFUL NATURE.

8. AS A SINLESS BABY, YOU ARE IN NEED OF A GOD TO KEEP YOU ALIVE; NOT IN NEED OF A SAVIOR UNTIL YOU GREW UP AND BECAME A SINNER BY YOUR OWN CHOICE.

9. THE BABY IS NOT A SINNER BECAUSE THE BABY DIED AT DELIVERY TIME OR WHENEVER.

IT IS FAR MORE IMPORTANT FOR US TO UNITE IN THE TRUTH, THAN TO UNITE IN ERROR.

That is why I wrote this book to counteract the error which is prevalent in the Protestant Churches including the Seventh-day Adventist Church.

....

CREATION – Gen. 1:1:31
ADAM AND EVE'S FALL
ABEL – DIED

The First Death is inherited from Adam.

JESUS' BIRTH
CALVARY

PROPHECY– REV. 13:16:18 = YOU CANNOT BUY OR SELL.
PROBATION CLOSES – 144,000 SEALED
JESUS – 2ND COMING
JESUS– 2RD COMING– WITH CITY– NEW JERUSALEM– REV. 21

FIRE
FIRE
FIRE

THE GREAT TRIBULATION

7 LAST PLAGUES – REV. 16

BOTTOMLESS PIT –
1,000 YEARS – REV. 20

ETERNAL DEATH TO THE WICKED INCLUDING SATAN AND HIS ANGELS

04 B.C.   31 A.D.   ???   ???

FIRST RESURRECT - ION.
THE RIGHTEOUS
THE WHEAT
THE SAVED
GOD'S REMNANT CHURCH

SECOND RESURRECT - ION.
THE WICKED - UNRIGHTEOUS
THE TARES
THE LOST

1. Abel was the first one to die <u>the First death</u> after Adam and Eve's sin. . . . Abel was killed by his own brother, Cain.

2. Adam later died *the First death* after living 930 years – (Genesis 5:1-5).

3. The <u>Second death which is eternal death</u> will take place for the wicked after the 1,000 years. (See the timeline above).

Prepared by: Metusela F. Albert.

Thank God for leading you to purchase this book and reading it with understanding.

Don't forget to share it with your friends to help them get out of those false teachings in the Protestant Churches.

Give God the glory. God bless. THE END.

Printed in the United States
by Baker & Taylor Publisher Services